MY MASTER'S DEGREE IS USELESS?!?!

HOW CHELSEA HANDLER, BOOZE, AND REALITY TV

TEACH **BETTER** MODERN-DAY BUSINESS LESSONS THAN THE LECTURE HALLS

WRITTEN BY

SONJA LANDIS

WHO HOLDS ONE OF THOSE USELESS MASTER'S DEGREES

(USA Today fact: 8 out of 10 people want to write a book. Guess where I stand on the issue...)

"My **worst fear**

is not being remembered when I'm dead."

-- Some Dead Guy

Landis, Sonja (2011-11-11). My Master's Degree is Useless?!?! Home Chelsea Handler, Booze, and Reality TV Teach Better Modern Day Business Lessons Better Than the Lecture Halls

Some content that appears in print may not be available in electronic books. Library of Congress Cataloging-In-Publication Data: Landis, Sonja ISBN 978-1-4636304-2-3 (ebk) 1. Entrepreneur. 2. Business. 3. Online Marketing. 4. Lifestyle. 5. Personal Development.

Media, San Diego, California

Printed in the United States of America

My Master's Degree is Useless?!?!

HOW CHELSEA HANDLER, BOOZE, AND REALITY TV

TEACH BETTER MODERN DAY BUSINESS LESSONS THAN THE LECTURE HALLS

Dedicated to my fellow dreamers... revolutionaries... Indigo Children... creative, inspired, and inspiring (or aspiring!) geniuses... the ones who feel that drive and determination deep in the soul to follow your own heart... the ones who aspire to change the world, or at least their part of it... the ones who bravely decide *mediocre* and *average* are just not enough for the gift of life we have on this planet... friends I was fortunate to meet, and friends I look forward to meeting in the future. (Maybe for Happy Hour....)

" Your time is limited, so don't waste it living someone else's life. Don't be trapped by dogma — which is living with the results of other people's thinking. Don't let the noise of others' opinions drown out your own inner voice. And most important, **have the courage to follow your heart and intuition.** They somehow already know what you truly want to become. Everything else is secondary."

- Steve Jobs

I happen to be writing this dedication on the day Steve Jobs passed away... It wasn't in here before today, but I just felt the need to pay tribute to one of my favorite dreamers, visionaries, geniuses, and mentors... and for any dreamers out there, sitting in a garage, I beg you to keep going. Keep moving forward. We need you! The world needs you. Imagine where we'd be if Steve Jobs had stopped, or settled for a desk job, or gave up... I mean, that's so whackadoodle, you can't *even imagine* where we'd be... !

Oct 5th, 2011. 5:27 PM PST

Table of Contents

FOREWARD AND **THANK YOUS**

This book has everything to do with the annually-popular notion of the New Year's Resolution, of which I whole-heartedly participate in. Often times I do not succeed in those resolutions, but I'm so optimistic it's downright adorable if I do say so myself. (And I do!) It's a Universal Truth with all people to want to improve on parts of life, big or small, to be the best person we can be. This book is about being better and moving towards greatness every single day, not just on NYE. (Plus I usually have a hang-over on Jan 1st, which is counterproductive to being awesome and great.) My personal belief is that a change in one aspect of your life can be deeply connected to changes in other aspects, and I see the root right around one's career choices in life. **When one chooses a career path and purpose, it is going to immediately affect their stress levels and fulfillment aspect of their life. Those 2 things impact one's health and fitness, emotional/mental well being, relationships, communication, education and development, lifestyle and finances, parenting style and involvement, and living arrangements. That's basically everything, if you're keeping score!** I wrote this book because I chose the wrong career for a long time, and went thru a LOT of personal pain, progress, and triumph in the process of finally finding the RIGHT one! I wanted to pass on any insight I could to inspire others, save them from some pitfalls, and streamline their success to get them to a state of awesomeness sooner, rather than later. The focus of this book is on career/business/passion/making money doing what you love, but the principles can be applied to any aspect of your life: weight loss, relationships, parenting, etc...

Here's the thing: too many people are lame. Stop being lame! You've got seriously kick-ass ideas to contribute to this planet... so do it! **All** people are really meant to be **creative, inspired,** and completely **fulfilled** & **passionate** about life. (Do you really think you were meant to work as a Customer Service Rep, answering phones all day?? Hells no!)

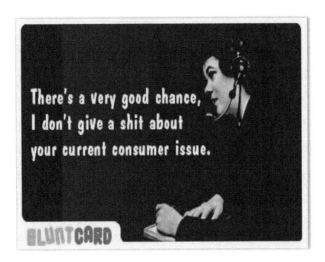

©BluntCard

All people are meant for greatness. **Some** people will make it happen. And **some others** will inspire others to find their own greatness...

I, **Sonja Landis,** am not really one of those people... j/k – I *TOTALLY* AM! I'm also smart enough to learn from them without being too terribly embarrassing or needy, successfully apply their ideas to my own life and career dreams, and now pass on the secrets, adventure, and wisdom for all. Enjoy!

THIS IS YOUR **LIFE.**
DO WHAT YOU LOVE,
AND DO IT OFTEN.
IF YOU DON'T LIKE SOMETHING, CHANGE IT.
IF YOU DON'T LIKE YOUR JOB, QUIT.
IF YOU DON'T HAVE ENOUGH TIME, STOP WATCHING TV.
IF YOU ARE LOOKING FOR THE LOVE OF YOUR LIFE, STOP;
THEY WILL BE WAITING FOR YOU WHEN YOU
START DOING THINGS YOU LOVE.
STOP OVER ANALYZING, ALL EMOTIONS ARE BEAUTIFUL.
WHEN YOU EAT, APPRECIATE
LIFE IS SIMPLE. EVERY LAST BITE.
OPEN YOUR MIND, ARMS, AND HEART TO NEW THINGS
AND PEOPLE, WE ARE UNITED IN OUR DIFFERENCES.
ASK THE NEXT PERSON YOU SEE WHAT THEIR PASSION IS,
AND SHARE YOUR INSPIRING DREAM WITH THEM.
TRAVEL OFTEN; GETTING LOST WILL
HELP YOU FIND YOURSELF.
SOME OPPORTUNITIES ONLY COME ONCE, SEIZE THEM.
LIFE IS ABOUT THE PEOPLE YOU MEET, AND
THE THINGS YOU CREATE WITH THEM
SO GO OUT AND START CREATING.
LIFE IS LIVE YOUR DREAM,
AND WEAR
SHORT. YOUR PASSION.

I got this off a friend's facebook mobile uploads and have been using it endlessly ever since... I have no idea where she got it, but I bet www.google.com is a good place to start.

ABOUT ME:

I have a Master's Degree, and it's not actually completely "useless." It made a lot of people proud, so that's cool... and about the only other thing it did was show me a path I absolutely could not and would not go down, which brought me on my real journey, to my true purpose and mission in life, here and now... with you! My Master's also focused on a lot of old-school, out-dated information in lecture halls... I actually remember one particularly mesmerizing class in which we disputed Union/Railroad Labor Law Case-Studies. Riveting, not to mention timely, right?!?!

Meanwhile, some kids from Harvard where blowing the world out of the water with Facebook and something called "Twitter" was emerging. "Mommy Bloggers" were making $40,000 a month "blogging" from home (now many many more of them make MORE than that – I'm saying MORE than $40K PER MONTH), but not this chick! No, not me. I was getting a Master's Degree in Business Development and Marketing, being groomed for the glitz and glamour of Corporate America 9 to 5... and I was A W E S O M E and going to get an A W E S O M E J O B because of it! (Plus was Entrepreneurship, like, totally, risky??? I wanted the "safety" of cubicles and "job security" by slaving away for someone else... didn't I?!?!?)

And I did get a corporate job, because of my degrees, and it was crappy. I despised it, the entire country was on the brink of this fun little recession we've all been going through, and I got canned. Luckily, I only got canned AFTER ending up in the Emergency Room with stress-induced kidney stones and anxiety attacks. Fun! I was 30.

Office Manager at Software Company (Chels

x@gmail.com>

the position I've been looking for!

Forget all the other candidates for Aviary, I am the BEST.

* Organizing shit? Check.
* Calling numbers and shit? Doublecheck.
* Customer support and shit? Mega-check.
* Faxing numbers and shit? MOTHERFLIPPING CHECK ALL OVER THAT.

Don't believe me? Check this shit out:

* I am devilishly handsome: I was Prom king two years in a row with
two different queens.
* I am ridiculously smart: I can solve any Rubiks cube in front of
your face with my magic fingers. I will bring one to prove it.
* I have pinpoint accuracy: I killed a hawk once with a ninja star
(sorry Aviary).
* I am good for office morale: When someone cries I am all sympathetic and shit.

Need my resume? Nope. Not when you got my FACTS!

* I am honorable: I am the son of a librarian and a capricorn.
* I am brave: I fight crime on weekends. I don't wear a cape yo that
shit is for PIMPS.
* I am dependable: Just call my name and I'll be there.

I'll pop in tomorrow to get my paperwork all signed up around 11 am.
No need for an interview, trust me you will love me. I got your
address from google, because my internet research skills are the shit.
I actually have been to a spa near your building before a few times so
I already know the area.

Love,
Roanald

PST. My favorite color is TOUPE because it rhymes with DOPE!!

(Hilarrrrr! I wish I had thought of this first.)

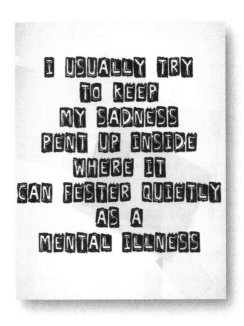

I USUALLY TRY TO KEEP MY SADNESS PENT UP INSIDE WHERE IT CAN FESTER QUIETLY AS A MENTAL ILLNESS

#TheSadTruth – a few years ago when I was in a job I hated.

Let's fast forward 3 years and a couple months... I now have a super-sweet-ass-kicking-bootcamp-style education in REAL WORLD business and life experiences, and a minor in Chelsea Handler, Reality TV, and Happy Hour... which gave me the freedom of living my passion as a full-time career (as an Artist, **which I always wanted to be**) and landed me in National Media Spotlights with Celebrity Clients. I have major corporate sponsorships and a pretty siiiiiick lifestyle in Southern California. I figured out how to live a life based on my values of fun, love, family, health, passion, vitality, and tons o' cashola. And I can show you how to do the same, in a streamlined way. I took the longer, bumpier path, but I know now I did it so I could write this book for all of you, and save you some time, trouble, and money. You're welcome. So let's go!

(Quick Legal Disclaimer, before we go on... the information presented here represents the views of the author/contributor(s) as of the date of publication. Conditions in the world change, and we all reserve the right to alter & update their opinions based on new conditions. This is all presented for informational purposes only... who has two thumbs and doesn't accept any liability for misuse of this info?? **This chick!** I did my best to verify everything provided, and any slights of people/organizations are unintentional... Now let's get back to the party, shall we?!?! This legal stuff is a real snooze to me.)

HAPPINESS DEPENDS UPON OURSELVES.

-ARISTOTLE

I'm a little sassy, a little saucy, and a little bit in-your-face with my logic and strategies. Besides English, I'm fluent in both profanity and sarcasm, and I speak a little White-Girl Spanglish too, which is always fun. I have a mean swagcabulary... I mean, considering my age and genetic make-up. I'm guessing if you saw the title of this book and are still hanging out with me anyway then you're ok with my style. I'm also seriously kind-hearted and love love love people, animals and the environment. So this is my blanket pre-apology for... nothing! I stand by everything in this book! (I do kinda apologize for thinking I'm funnier than I probably am.) I tend to think myself a bit of a comedic genius, much to the chagrin of the people I spend the most time with, who would give me an *"ehhhh..."*

EXPECT THIS:

Creative, proven, effective, step-by-step business ideas (some

Life Lessons too) and advice for YOU to take ACTION on and move from Point A, which is sucky, or close to sucky, to Point B, which is looking & feeling more like being amazing, inspir**ed**, inspir**ing**, successful, rich, and drinking Peach Sangrias on the beach. Are you with me on this, peeps??

You mustn't be afraid
to dream a little bigger,
darling!

Let's get started. We've got a lot to cover together & a lot to do. I guarantee you're going to be better, smarter, and have new perspective on things in some (hopefully MANY!) ways by the end of this book. I'm going to try and make you laugh. I'm going to try and inspire you to greatness and take steps outside of your comfort zone for the benefit of YOUR personal growth. And I'm going to do it all with a pinch of super-honest-reality-check attitude. If I were too nice and cookie-cutter typical, you wouldn't put anything into practice or question your current situation enough. The goal is to DO BIG THINGS, not just read about how to do it, homey. You've probably been "thinking" about your life and dreams too long...

(If you haven't really even thought about it yet, oy vey!, well then we've got a lot of fun ahead of us!) It's time to DO SOMETHING ABOUT IT. Please keep your hands inside the coaster at all times. No flash photography.

WHY DO I CARE??:

"And **why**, exactly, do you care if **I'm** lame and half-assing it in life or rich, fabulous, and happy??" you might ask...

First of all, rich, fabulous and happy people are better for the planet. Better energy, juju, moxie, mojo, karma, and creativity go into the Universe, which is good for me, good for my son who is growing up with YOUR kids, and good for the overall flow of life. Rich, fabulous, and happy people tend to be super generous, and a lot of excellent Charity/Foundation/Research/Goodness happens because of donations from these kinds of peeps. If you're lame, sad, and slugging it out in your own life and with some shitty job you hate, you can't be a problem-solver and big contributor to the greater good as easily. You've got your own issues, if you get what I'm sayin'. (I say this with all the empathy in my heart, cuz I was there and I know what it feels like.) I truly believe in my entire body and mind that if you're reading this, you've

got much bigger plans for your life than middle-management at Cogswell Cogs. **WE ALL DO!!!**

Don't ask what the world needs. Ask what makes **you** come alive, and go do it.

Because what the world needs is people who have come alive.

- Howard Thurman

The other reason I care is because like I said, I've been where you are, and it's the pits. I was so beat down, depressed, and unfilled when I was in the trenches, at war with myself, my own job, my guilt for wanting more when I should've been "happy" with a "good job." I was exhausted, overwhelmed, unfulfilled, and numb... if you feel any of those things too, I want to help it stop.

BANKSY

Killer Street Artist. British Dude. Watch *EXIT THRU THE GIFT SHOP* movie for more on him.

I ended up in the hospital with kidney stones and anxiety attacks at 30 years old. No bueno. I hadn't slept well in months, and all day long was pumping my body up with caffeine to make up for it. Also no bueno. I was s l o w w w w l y digging my own grave. The biggest no bueno of all! Let's talk about stress for a moment. I was in constant stress at a job I hated, suffocating my own happiness every single day, and fighting my inner demons (namely guilt, since I had such a "nice" house and "good" job... picture perfect, white-picket-fence-style!).

Here's some of the skinny on stress:

- It *can* make you skinny, but it can also make you fat. (*I've experienced both.*)
- It interferes with sleep and causes insomnia
- It signals the brain to release chemicals that often INCREASE feelings of physical PAIN in the body... specifically headaches, backaches, and chronic joint/neck pain
- It can cause infertility in women
- It can cause infertility in men
- It causes **PREMATURE BALDNESS** in both men AND WOMEN *(ummmm, no thanks!)*
- It causes skin problems like zits and rashes *(attractive!)*

- **It clogs up your pipes:** causing gastrointestinal disorders such as ulcers, lower abdominal cramps, colon problems, and irritable bowel syndrome (IBS)... (*always a welcome situation at parties and social events!*)
- Heart disease is the number one killer of American **women**. High blood pressure, heart attacks, heart palpitations, and stroke all are considered stress-related cardiovascular conditions.
- Stress alters your brain functioning, decision making, and goal setting ability for short term stuff, and accelerates the aging (not good) of the brain. You can transplant a heart and stay the same person. You can't transplant a brain and say the same thing. Take care of your noodle!
- It's a real downer in bed! Stress can cause erectile dysfunction for dudes and extreme vaginal dryness for chicks. (*If stress hadn't caused depression yet, it certainly would with **THIS** one!*)
- Stress sincerely kills people, and it does it slowly & miserably... and it **was happening to me.**

(Source: www.Google.com, duh! And **everyone** knows **everything** on Google is truth! www.Health.About.Com/stress)

As breath is the substance of life,

stress is the substance of death.

- Dr. Ben Johnson, M.D.

So with all those fun facts about stress, I decided to take my over-nighter and outpatient kidney stone procedure as a wake-up call. The dialog went a little like this:

Universe: Alert to Sonja! Alert to Sonja! This is your LIFE and you are fucking it up! Please stop now!

Me: OK. I get it. This stress and anxiety hurts and it sucks. Let's be friends instead!

Universe: Now you're talkin'…

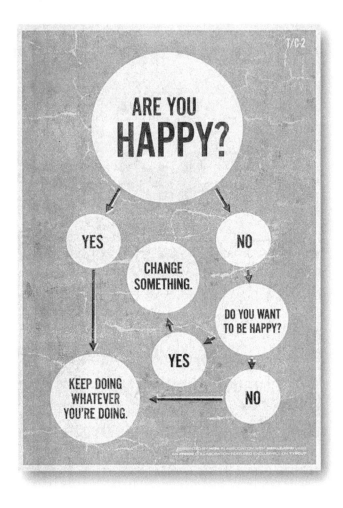

Do you value life?

Then waste not **time**, for that is **the stuff of which life is made**.

- Benjamin Franklin

I'll tell you the whole story and be totally transparent with you, so you can learn from my mistakes. Please don't judge me. I also sometimes forget to spell check and I do cuss, so please don't judge me on those points either. Cool?!?! Ok, so I wish I had someone break it down for me like this when I was figuring it all out, but I will high-five myself on making the really tough changes I needed to, moving through any fear and doubt to become the person I was meant to be, and coming out as one of those rich, fabulous, and happy people on the other side! It's all worth it, friends, and if you think it might not be, slap yourself. For reals. So many people **cling** (which is, let's be perfectly clear here, not a good look on ANYONE) to having a "safe, responsible, a.k.a shitty soul-sucking" job... what... are you clinging to?!?! If you're not rich, fulfilled, and passionate about your life or career yet, then read on, you sexy thing you... we'll get there! Like Kim Kardashian's butt, this lifestyle is real, and it is fantastic. Unlike Kim Kardashian's butt, anyone can have it.

© <u>www.BluntCard.com</u> – This company is freaking genius.

(LOL. That's funny.)

MY QUICK TIMELINE, IN A NUTSHELL:

Born – Raised – Middle Class – Midwest

Nothing huge, nothing small here. Mostly fabulously ordinary and as good as can be for anyone. Lovely, really. Normal teenage angst. Smoked some weed, but not much… seriously only a couple times. Drank & partied with my friends at keggers and went skinny-dipping in too many lakes and pools because of it. Skipped school sometimes. Played sports. Zero pregnancies. Graduation.

College – Arizona State University – Go Devils!

I'm on fire, and the world is mine. I'm broke, but so are most kids in college. I'm happy, but I'm changing my Major. Often. More than most. I secretly want to study Art and Interior Design, **but I'm afraid to fail**.

Plus everyone knows that's a "flaky" type of career and I'll be broke forever and end up cutting my own ear off. Soooo, to protect my own ego, I pick other Majors that I don't *really* love, and then I can keep my **real** dream safe. And hidden. Yeah, that makes total sense… let's go with that plan. Stayed away from drugs. Drank a lot. Went thru many fake IDs. Zero pregnancies. Graduation.

Slew Of Jobs I Wasn't Very Good At – Part of the Path – A Learning Experience

I joined the USAF because someone else thought it was a good idea. I got to travel, saw beautiful places and things; saw horrible places and things. Met great people; met idiots. I'm a pretty happy person overall, but deep down I was never ever ever satisfied, excited, fulfilled or enjoying my job in the Air Force. I start letting people see my Artwork, and then start selling some pieces, and I'm getting great feedback. The thing I hear the most is "I never even *knew* you were an Artist!" (I'm starting to see a flaw in my original – and stupid – plan of keeping my dream hidden…). Got my oh-so-useful-and-impressive Master's Degree. Had a baby. Left the Air Force (7+ years). Got a crappy Financial Advisor job I *hated*. Left there, and got another one at a Bank that I *loathed*. Ended up in the hospital with those really fun stress-related medical problems. Got fired in the recession. Moved to Southern California and finally decided to become an Artist. Got scared and took another Corporate Finance job I *despised*, working for a complete Pervy McPervert. Was miserable. Was introduced to Network Marketing (or MLM – Multi Level Marketing) and made not one damn dime. I wasn't fired up about any of it, or nutritional supplements or anything… however, it was a ginormous turning point in my "education" because I was introduced to so much knowledge about Personal Development, Attitude, Vision, and Lifestyle.
Like the real-deal type of lifestyle I was craving. I began learning, researching, and really listening to my own voice. Then, I went to sling Insurance, and was most miserable of all. This was NOT how it was supposed to be going out here in the land of fruits and nuts! (i.e. California, and I love ya!) **BUT!!!** The whole entire time I was learning and building my passion, my dream, and my Art Career all along. It was tiring and draining, but I was ready to finally breakthrough. Yipeeeee!

LaCK OF
passion
is FaTaL

Personal Trials Along the Way – I Know It's Hard – Don't Buy Your Own Excuses

I'm not telling you the road to riches, abundance, freedom & happiness is easy. It's hard, but totally worth it, without a doubt. You've got a lot o' shit you deal with. I did too! But if I can do it, you really can as well. I got divorced and became a single-mom on this path. That's hard, but it was the right decision. I wasn't going to be able to grow in that relationship. I was going to suffocate. I'm not an advocate of divorce, unless it's the absolute correct choice, and I do believe a lot of times, it is. Bummer, I know. What I've learned about divorce is that it's crazy expensive and financially/emotionally devastating, even when it's as cordial as can be... like ours pretty much was. But I also know I was able to grow into the person I was meant to become, and so is he, and we are both better/different people because of the experience. It still sucks, and I'm not going to sugarcoat it! We had to short-sell our house, a super-nice house in a gorgeous neighborhood, in the recession. We lost a boat-load of money, and even though our divorce was fairly amicable, it was still expensive. I filed for bankruptcy, effed up my credit, and had to borrow another boat-load of money. "Boat" meaning the "Titanic." It wasn't my shining star of all moments, believe me, but I knew it was the path. I had great family, friends, and a support system who wanted me out of that marriage and VERY MUCH wanted me to succeed. I read **A LOT** of great books, went to seminars, and really developed as a person into who I was meant to become. (I have a list of recommended resources and books/people I found extremely helpful and amazing throughout and listed at the end of this book, and I encourage you all to start the path, wherever you might be.)

Mistakes are part of the dues one pays for a **full life**.

- Sophia Loren

I don't want to get to the end of my life and find that I just lived the length of it. I want to have lived the width of it as well.

——— DIANE ACKERMAN ———

THE PAST IS PRACTICE.

My friends and I are here to happily introduce you to your future.

We're here to say:

Go ahead! Be the Fruitloop in a world full of Cheerios!

At least 11,486,932 other things happened in my life, but this isn't all about me, darling... it's about you, too, and how to learn from my goods, bads, and uglies. You'll get little snippets scattered throughout the rest of the book when they illustrate a good lesson, but in the spirit of honesty and with respect to everyone's time, please realize there were other accomplishments, catastrophes, Happy Hours and hangovers involved with the aforementioned timeline of events. And if you were with me on any of those, thanks. I bet we had fun!

Careful in casting out your demons lest you cast out the best part of yourself!

- Nietzsche

Here is my disclaimer on Copyright and legal stuff. I'm not a lawyer, I don't have a lawyer, and I don't have all these editors and big fancy publishing houses telling me what to do and how to do it. What I DO have is a message, and a good one, and I've worked really hard to provide it to other people with this book and my coaching programs for Small Businesses and Entrepreneurs. I use a lot of pictures and images in this book to make people laugh, prove a point, and create this book in a style that I would like to read. I've tried my best to give the proper credit and point you in the direction of the source to find more about their work or products or whatever. Most of this shit I've pulled off the internet, so I'm basically like Google in that I have a ton of research, knowledge, wisdom, experience, and insight... and I'm doing my best to give it to you in a useful format and help you apply it to make your life better. I want to make you laugh while I do that, because, well, I like to laugh. A LOT. It's not my intent to claim Copyright or infringe on anything that's not from my own noggin. I've learned a lot from other people, and now I show others the way based on my own application, mistakes, and successes from the years I've poured into my own career. Everything I do, in every way I do it, comes from the intention of laughter, fun, and much love and benefit for all. I want the people who come in contact with me and with my book to be better, smarter, and happier because of our connection. That's my intent.

I'd also like to add here a disclaimer on Religion, or lack-there-of if that's your case. I have my beliefs; you have yours. Please as a general rule, insert whatever or whomever you choose in place of the word "God" or "Universe" or "Source" or "Spirit." Mmmm-kay??? Let's all just accept and respect one another's thoughts and modify the language as appropriate. Please don't write me about Religion. This would be my response:

© www.SomeECards.com

IMPORTANT **THANK YOUS!**

My Parents, Brother, and Family, including my Ex's Family, who've all remained Family even after the divorce. My friends. My mentors. People whom I've never met, but through their books and wisdom have taught me so much, and I wouldn't be here without them. MY SON!!! I love him so much, and love that we teach EACHOTHER, inspire EACHOTHER, love EACHOTHER, and learn from EACHOTHER. It's not just one-way. He is amazing, smart, funny, loving, kind, and gorgeous in every way possible. Special

thanks to my guy, who IS my strength, support, and warrior/defender/protector of my dreams along the way... present tense, because it's just the beginning. He thinks I'm smarter than I am, prettier than I am, and funnier than I am... and believe me, there's nothing better in the whole world than that. <<swoon!>>

www.lookonthebrightside.uk.com

And also to all those along the way who taught me who I *don't* want to be... that's not a negative thing in any way, shape, or form. It takes all kinds in this world, and I am just acknowledging differences, without which I wouldn't be able to find the right path for me. Much much much LOVE to you all!

To Sugar Free Mountain Dew Amp, which undoubtedly reeks havoc on my body and internal organs in many unknown ways, but without you this book would not have reached completion, probably ever. Was I all tweaked out till 3 and 4 am for several nights that last week of writing?? You betcha. But the book got done, didn't it?!?! All for you guys! (Don't worry, I did a good *Crazy Sexy Diet* 21-day cleanse ala Kris Carr after I finished writing this book & weaned off the crack-in-a-can as quickly as possible...)

I want to thank a very good college friend of mine, who recently gave me the BEST compliment ever: "**Sonja**, I'm so glad you were so bad at your other jobs, cuz now you really just get to be you and because of that, **you're gonna inspire the world**." (Swoon!) Maybe not the *world* (yet), but, I mean, like, *half the world* would be cool...

UPDATE! I got another one-of-the-greatest-ever-compliments-of-all-time from a different friend. "I called you because you make me feel good when I feel like shit." To that I say, I'm happy about it, my friend. XOXO

(Hmmm... Come to think of it, I hope this person doesn't mean in the ultra-elitist way I watch those crazy assholes on *Hoarders* or *Locked Up Abroad* or *Freaky Eaters* and feel better about myself. Does this person call me cuz I'm a hot mess?? Am I a hot mess?? Ehhh. Whatever. Party on!)

AN **EXTRA SPECIAL THX** TO GUEST WRITERS AND PROFESSIONAL PARTNERS:

To all the fabulous guest writers and contributors, who were asked to be a part of this book because of the amazing and unique contributions you make in our world. We all need to know more people like you! I'm glad you're here. I'm humbled, grateful, inspired by both your input in here & your work out there.

thankyou**thankyou**thankyou**thankyou**thankyou**thankyou**thankyou**thankyou**thankyou**thankyou

RULES OF **ENGAGEMENT:**

1. **Choose** to be open-minded and receptive. That's not super easy at first; it took me a while to really get the hang of this one too, but you'll get there. **Choose** to get there. No one ever complained their way to success and riches, or happiness for that matter. Think about it.

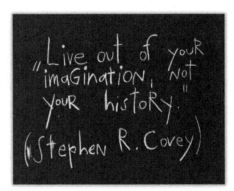

www.pinterest.com

2. Be nice. I try to be funny, and I do poke a little fun at others, especially at myself and my experiences. I like to laugh, and funny things happen all around me all the time, plus I try my hardest to see the humor and lesson in every situation. <u>It's all in good fun and used to inspire action for you</u>, so let's all **choose** to be nice. I'm really a very nice person, in spite of the sporadic and wicked sarcasm, lol.

3. **Believe in yourself**. If something here TOTALLY goes against what you personally believe to be true, then ignore it. Move on to the next part. Practice and put into action everything else that does make sense to you. I'm not mad! I'm just here, talking like me, walking like me, and being me. My message is: give this life all you've got and put YOUR specific contribution into the world in the easiest, fastest, most efficient, and most lucrative way possible.

www.beautiful.tumblr.com

4. Know that when I use the words "rich," "wealth/wealthy," or "abundance" it actually **DOES NOT** only mean money. Although I will show you how to leverage your time and efforts to put a ton of money in the bank, and I encourage people to do great and wise things with money in as many generous ways as possible, I don't want you to be a millionaire if that's not what you want. Each of those words mean prosperity manifesting in many areas of your life, **most importantly your health** (physical and emotional) **and soul** (as in heart &). As for me, I want to be RICH in my health, heart, soul AND have oodles of dollars in the bank because that equals options, choices, freedom, and generous actions for me. And gorgeous shoes. I certainly won't deny or apologize for that. (You may shoe-gasm now)

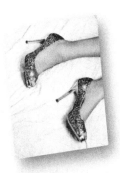  

© www.Louboutin.com (I imagine… I got them off of www.Pinterest.com)

5. **Choose** to take action. Even when it's scary. When you feel resistance, it means it's probably ringing true for you. That will probably trigger fear which signals the need to protect yourself. That equals more resistance (procrastination and inaction), and you retreat to "safety." Then you're clinging again to something you're not super stoked about, and it's a mean little cycle. So here's what you do: Acknowledge the fear. Acknowledge it's there for your ego's protection. Then **choose** to take a little step forward; a mini-step at first. You're building a great big wall of amazing-ness... just move one brick at a time, making sure it's laid straight and strong. Soon you'll see the wall emerging, and you'll be building it effortlessly, happily, energetically. I promise!

The way to get started
is to stop talking and begin doing.
- Walt Disney

6. Please try each exercise. If it feels totally in-authentic to you **after** you've given it a shot, then move on to something else. When I ask action questions, for you to think about and use as a building block, please don't come up with answers like "nothing," "I'm not," "I can't," "I shan't." (Does anyone still use that word? No one that would ever read *this* book, I can tell you that...) Point is, **give yourself permission** to really answer each question. It's just you and me right

now; we're not on Letterman. No one is watching and judging you, so really give this stuff a chance!

7. You are allowed to want things, and don't ever let anyone make you feel guilty about that! Other people's rules do not need to apply to you, and vice versa. Give yourself permission to want what you want and be willing to work for it. (A good strategy isn't really to want Jimmy Choos and expect a rich dude to buy them for you. That's kind of bitchy. If you want those Choos, figure out how to be rich, fabulous, and happy and get them for yourself... Much better plan!)

FACT: IT IS OK FOR ME TO HAVE EVERYTHING I WANT.

FACT: IT IS OK FOR YOU TO HAVE EVERYTHING YOU WANT, TOO.

Give yourself permission, then be willing to achieve <u>AND receive</u>!

NO GUILT ATTACHED

CHAPTER ONE: IF THAT IDIOT SNOOKI CAN DO IT, SO CAN YOU

OK. I use the term "idiot" here loosely, because Snooki makes bank and figured out how to KEEP making bank, much longer than *anyone* in this entire Universe would have thought. Or she was smart enough to find an agent who does this for her, and smart enough to take his/her advice. Either way, chick has a LOT of dolla dollas, Press, Media, and material goods coming her way. I do use the term "idiot" because her approach and fame is so in-authentic and painful for me to watch it makes me wince.

My main message to everyone is this:

Be rich, fabulous, and happy while living your passion in a way you'll be eternally proud of as your legacy and contribution while you were here on Earth.

As for me, I try to be wasted with my undies around my ankles as **INFREQUENTLY** as possible... in public, anyways. So Snooki and her antics, indeed, make me cringe, label, gossip, and poke fun. (I'm only human... I put my cute panties on one leg at a time just like you.)

I'm not terribly shy, and I'm completely willing to put myself all out there in a **non-Snooki kind of way**, and I encourage EVERYONE to do the same. Seriously. I don't suggest you do anything Snooki-like for money, however it is important to note that she has book deals, media attention, Late Show appearances, commercials, a new "flip-flop" and "wedge sandal" shoe line (with pickles and leopard prints... I couldn't make that up if I *wanted* to), and bank **$$$**. She's syndicated, for God's sake! Point being: If that idiot Snooki can do it, and put all her, ummmmm, ~~talent~~ ~~ideas~~ personality (??) into the world, then mygoodnessgraciousgreatballsoffire SO CAN YOU! Please, if you ever ever ever ever doubt yourself, think of Snooki's line of flip-flops with pickle-patterns on them. Please.

For the record, I actually have a lot of respect for the way she's handled her business. America loves a train wreck, and she never disappoints. She is certainly the antithesis of skinny, leggy, beautiful, and fit Hollywood, and people are absolutely DRAWN to it. (She's a "Purple Cow", which we're going to talk about here soon, and everyone else is brown cow brown cow brown cow, same same same...) She writes NY Times Bestsellers, she is an E! THS (True Hollywood Story), and she has an actual empire that she's built... that is an amazing accomplishment few will ever attain.... I gotta give the ole' Snooksters props for that! Recently I heard her say she truly wants to step away from the I-fell-on-my-face-drunk-in-the-sand-and-everyone's-seen-my-naked-ass Snooki and continue more as Nicole Polizzi, and I could genuinely feel here sincerity about that. I'm looking forward to seeing the development, and I asked Snooki to be a guest contributor to the book (although I had already picked the name of this chapter, which probably didn't go over so well), but apparently she was way too busy buying Prada and rear-ending police officers in Italy. Oh well, cest la vie. I know that's French, but it fits here anyways.

YOUR TAKE AWAY: If Snooki (and a whole bunch of other idiots not pointed out here, but all over Bravo TV) can create abundance by being a knuckle-head, then I can certainly do it by being amazing, awesome, intelligent, and possibly ridiculously good-looking... (I don't know, I haven't seen you, but that might apply and certainly never hurts...). If Snooki can do it, so can I. If Snooki can do it, so can I. If Snooki can do it, so can I.

ONE MORE TAKEAWAY: Sonja Landis doesn't really think Snooki is a complete idiot, or anyone else on Bravo or Jersey Shore or anything else... (Well, I mean, *kind of* she does, but in the spirit of kindness and humanity and all that junk, she doesn't *really*...). That was a weird disclaimer! OK, so Sonja is actually a nice person and is just trying to be funny, and when she uses the term "idiot" et. al. it's to make a point and/or make me laugh. Got it.

You don't get what you **want,**

you get what you BELIEVE.

- Oprah Winfrey

Let's start with your belief system, like deep deep deep down what you're telling yourself and your relationship with money. (I know, I know... you've done "The Secret" and you're totally squared-away here, good to go... but just humor me for the rest of this chapter.)

Everyone starts out with small steps, and everyone is unsure and nervous in the beginning of anything. Everyone! Some people work through it and show it in more or less obvious ways, but this is a primitive human response of fight or flight, and it's present in every single person at first. Have you ever seen a famous movie star's old audition tapes?? Horrible! **But they kept going, kept improving.** Nuff said. Here's the important part: When you're in this vulnerable stage, recognize that your dreams, goals, ideas, ambitions, and actions are fragile. Protect them. If someone makes you feel bad about them or about only taking small steps in the beginning, be careful how much you include those people as you proceed. Eventually you will be a mega-powerhouse of momentum, a force to be reckoned with, and be able to easily bypass anyone's negativity and doubt. But at first, it's hard. Be on the lookout for these people, who may be closest to you, love you to no end, and have the best intentions for you... sometimes the people who want to keep you in that "safety-zone" in life can do the most (often unintentional) damage. You are the protector and warrior of your dreams right now. Choose wisely who you let in at first, young Jedi.

I'm so excited to introduce you to some interesting and inspiring people throughout this book, and I've asked them to contribute words of wisdom and their individual perspective and stories for the greater good of my readers... each of them are **creative** and **talented** in their own field, with their own unique contribution, in numerous different forms of Artistry and Business. The first is

Miss Sylvia J, brand new Pop Princess with her hit single *"Wild Girls"* available on iTunes and on her album (coming soon).

"You can't stuff a great life into a small dream."

"

Passion, patience, and perseverance. I was near the end of my rope with music, frustrated and feeling isolated... I sat defeated in my brother's real estate office in Detroit, tears flooding my eyes. I was about to give up, yet couldn't imagine the bleak future of a "normal" 9 to 5 when I was so passionate about my dream... Music made me feel alive. The thought of doing anything else made me feel dead inside. I believed in myself, but not everyone understood my drive... until fate (and Craigslist) brought me to my (now) Producer, Mr. Emerson Windy AKA Eric Reese AKA ReesePiece, CEO of Pearl Harbor Entertainment.

I don't know if it was my last shot or not (and thankfully I don't have to ever find out!), but I contacted him and flew out to his SoCal studio. He's confident, patient, and talented. He helped define and hone my sound, style, and niche, made me believe I could be great, and collaborated projects and negotiations to get MY distribution deal with Universal Records. He gave me a shot at music when I was at rock bottom, thinking it was over before it had even begun. How could an underdog like me, who has faced so much adversity, negativity, and "no"s, ever become an International Pop Star? And here I stand, all Lady Gaga style, on, ya know, **my very own** *Edge of Glory*... Never let anyone underestimate you, and stick with those who believe in your abilities, because they are the ones who will help you shine.

"Courage is not defined by those who fought and did not fall,

but by those who fought, fell, and rose again."

With my Producer at my side, I continue to fight for my spot at the top. I'll keep fighting, falling, rising again... a Phoenix from the ashes, as many times as it takes. I have been actively pursuing this crazy career for 10 years. 10 years! I knew I had to make sacrifices, put in the time, and keep fighting for my dream. I wouldn't change a thing because it made me who I've become -

ambitious, determined, dedicated, and completely focused on my goals. It's better to know what you want (no matter how big and difficult), and fight for it till your last breath, then not know and settle for what someone else tells you you "should be" doing. Listen to your own heart!

"Success is a matter of hanging on after others have let go".

I also give it all I've got. I stuck by my dreams and went after them, even when everyone told me I couldn't do it. I always knew if I wasn't willing to put in 120%, someone else was. In my wildest dreams, I'm achieving my goals... but I'm actually awake!

Getting to the place "they" all told you was off limits is about the highest degree of happiness you can reach! Your dreams become a reality, your hunger for that glory is being fed, and the passion & desire you have for what you love to do is fulfilled. Time means nothing when you're doing what you love.

"

Coolest part?? We all have that potential! And that's all she wrote... !

***

What's your Inner Framework??

Your sense of confidence, which allows you to move through fear, choose courage and empowerment, and ignite a state of creative **flow** in progress and development. It is a path of personal growth, not to fully *change* you, but actually *FIND* the real you that kinda got lost in the shuffle and struggle and stories – LIES – of "I can't"s and "You can't"s. It's both your Foundation (the key to building something that lasts a long time), and your Structure (the actions, practices, and fundamentals that build upon each other, creating support and strength for what you're building).

INNER FRAMEWORK = FOUNDATION + STRUCTURE

When I get sad, I stop being sad. I start being awesome instead.

True Story.

We need your Inner Framework rock-solid, not wobbly. **So you need to address any of your junk.** I'm talking about any of those wounds and painful experiences of the past, emotional/physical abuse that developed, insidious & destructive stories you tell yourself about "worthiness." Let's stop. **Everyone is worthy.** Everyone is not only **WORTHY**, but actually **EXPECTED and REQUIRED** to do great things! You were created and placed on this Earth at this time to creatively contribute to the world. When a person doesn't do this, they start to suffocate and develop deep feelings of depression. Some people start to question their own existence... you weren't put here by a Higher Power to just exist. You aren't doing life justice by merely "existing."

Stop exhisting. Start living.

I mean living life fully awake, in the full potential of who you are, with all of your senses and intuition working together, harmoniously.

BEING AWAKE, ENGAGED, ALIVE, INSPIRED, ACTIVE

VS.

NUMB, OVERWHELMED, DISCONNECTED, EXHAUSTED

If you don't love what you do... If you don't love your life... (and I mean **LOVE!**) If you're not totally passionate and at peace in what you do, you will **NEVER** be in a state of flow...

Flow occurs when you have both present contentment AND a vision you're excited about moving toward in the future. Flow engages & fuels you to make an impact with your life. Flow moves forward. Flow is part of alignment (which is an important concept we'll continue to address). You have the choice to be part of your flow. You have the choice right now.

I know some people feel a little silly about Affirmations and Visualization techniques. The thing is, they work, and you just have to keep trying them. Most people get bent, frustrated, and worried about stuff, and **that's** what they focus on morning/noon/night... then blame Affirmations and Visualization for not working. In the book, *The Answer*, by John Assaraf and Murray Smith, they have a great exercise to produce Affirmations, Visualization, and Ideal Client Manifestation for your business goals, whatever they may be. Here are mine, and you are free to use or expand on them as you wish. It wasn't easy to stick to the repetition at first, but I now have a habit of waking up grateful and saying some silent affirmations (**BEFORE** I check my Smartphone!), expressing gratitude and saying affirmations for experiences during the day and before appointments/phone calls, and doing the same before I fall asleep at night. Because of the practice, I am much more calm, present in the moment, and appreciative for all I have. I breathe deeper, communicate better, and embrace all situations (even crappy ones) for learning experiences on the journey. Before I made this a habit I was much more reactionary. Now I feel more confident and proactive (not like the facewash), and I know the Affirmations have a lot to do with that. Oh, and some of mine are the same as John Assaraf's. He said we could use his, like I just said to you, and I totally did on some.

- *I am a creative genius and I use my wisdom daily*
- *I give myself permission to be wealthy and powerful*
- *I consistently attract all the right people to help me grow my business*
- *I have all the talent, intelligence, creativity, and resources I need, right now, to grow my businesses and career into Multi-Million Dollar International companies*
- *I am calm, succinct, happy, and likeable when being interviewed and presenting*
- *I always have enough time to accomplish my daily goals*
- *I travel safely and meet the most amazing, friendly people everywhere I go*
- *I pay all my bills on time **and with gratitude** for the services I receive*
- *My businesses are, right now, filled with prosperity, abundance, and my ideal clients*
- *Learning new things comes easily to me*
- *I am someone who takes action and gets things done*
- *I have the best of intentions for all people and living things in all that I do*
- *I always have clarity of purpose, focus, inspiration, and creativity*
- *Making money excites and energizes me!*
- *I love sharing my work with others and living an abundant lifestyle because of it*
- *Being afraid is a normal feeling in the face of something new... I feel the doubt and do it anyway, and I triumph every time*
- *I learn new things each day and can achieve whatever I set my mind to*
- *I use my wealth, prosperity, and energy very wisely*
- *I receive and give back all the best things in the world every day*

When things GO WRONG. (And sometimes they do.)

Your **strong Inner Framework** will kick in and be able to support you and see you to the other side. When things go wrong it sucks, and it's a test, but they go wrong for everyone at some point. So go back to those Affirmations and have faith in knowing **it really does work out in the end... If it's not working out right now, then it's not the end.** But here's the thing: God is loving, and not cruel. He/She doesn't set you up to permanently fail. God doesn't help you discover your path and then not give you a way to get there. So calm down, breathe deeply, and keep moving forward, focusing on what you *can* control at the moment.

For I know the plans I have for **you**, declares the Lord.

Plans to prosper you and not to harm you,

plans to give you a hope and a future.

Jeremiah 29:11

Please… just take the message and don't worry about the "God" parts if you don't want to…

Any Higher Power you believe in is **guiding YOU for greater good**, not pain. Plus you can always have a little drink, and things seem better already!

CHAPTER **TWO:** TAKE THE ROAD

Everything tells me that I am about to make a wrong decision,

but making mistakes is just a part of life.

What does the world want of me?

Does it want me to take no risks, to go back to where I came from

because I didn't have the courage to say **yes** to life?

- Paulo Coehlo

True Story:

I'm athletic, an adventurer and nature-lover... but in a semi-moderate kind of way, to say the least... not the "extreme" type, ya know?!?! So one gorgeous Autumn afternoon when I was asked to go for a 3ish hour mountain-bike ride up a steep, albeit breathtaking, peak in Northern Arizona, I was totally game! I was in killer shape if I do say so myself, and excited to go.

That "ride" turned into a 20 *minute* ride and a **6 hour and 40 minute hike/perilous climb** up this hellacious trail in which I literally had to either carry or leave my mountain bike. I was broke and in college, and my bike was sweet and expensive. I chose to carry it. I'm not big, but I am deceptively strong. This, however, was way past acceptable, or safe. I know I can't completely paint the picture for you of how dangerous this was, but believe me, I thought me and my Cannondale were going to plummet to our deaths more times than I'd like to admit. My palms are sweating now just remembering it. I was pretty effing miserable. I was in pain and inwardly complaining/outwardly cussing part (most) of the way. We were tired, hungry, and stuck. It was too dangerous to climb down, yet every step up the peak was THAT much higher if I did fall. I very seriously and secretly asked God that if I was going to fall, to break my neck and not let me lay there defenseless to be eaten by mountain lions. This 7+ hour vertical endeavor with a cumbersome bicycle on my back was not even a little bit of the 3 hour ride I had envisioned...

Guess what. I made it, bitches! It was a miraculous view, beautiful, and glorious. I was so thankful I almost wept. If I wasn't so dehydrated and could've actually produced tears I probably would have. I felt like a champion, thru-and-thru and immediately forgot about how miserable I was and how many f-bombs I dropped along the way. I looked and felt like I had been to hell and back, but I was PROUD. I breathed in all that fresh, cool mountain air and filled my lungs with LIFE, baby!!! Ahhhhh! I felt FANTASTIC!!! Thank Jesus, Mary and Joseph, Buddha, Allah, Lady Gaga, and Cher... The climb was isolating and character-building... it was as close to my ascent to Mt. Everest as I was ever going to get,

because I'm not doing that shit ever again! Still, on top of the mountain, I thought smugly to myself, "I did what so few people have actually done! I did something pretty gnarly today!" That's when I noticed a young kid standing behind me a ways. An *interesting* kid... he clearly had Down's Syndrome. I saw more kids... an entire *slew* of kids, actually, most disabled or mentally handicapped in some way. I saw families picnicking, playing games, running and laughing. Wha??? I see a bus. *A BUS??* Wha???

Turns out there was a ROAD several hundred yards away from where I was risking life and limb (no exaggeration), tarzan-ing myself to blisters and performing near-death acrobatic maneuvers to get me and that titanium-alloy nightmare to safety.

Life Lesson: Take the road. Dummy. You could've seriously died out there.

Business Lesson: Take the road. Dummy. You can seriously die out there.

I wasn't prepared, I never checked a map, I didn't have a plan or the right supplies, I was doing something dangerous, and the other person with me was A) doing the exact same thing, as unprepared and in as much danger as me and 2) an idiot for a lot of other reasons we won't discuss here. (Just kidding – you're not *really* an idiot (I guess), plus I doubt you're reading my book anyways...) Just please listen to this wisdom: Take the road. It's just as pretty at the top, it takes less time and energy, and you have a significantly lower chance of dying. That's what I've got for you right here. A road & a map of what worked, what didn't, and all I've learned along the way. Years and years of knowledge, research, and experts; a Master's Degree in Business Development and Marketing (not *really* "useless," but we'll get to that part later!); and tens of thousands of dollars of education and real-world experience – just for YOU, vixen! Let's continue, this is fun!

This "road & map" I'm oh-so-cleverly alluding to is our prep work. We need to begin in the right way, so you don't ever end up with a Cannondale on YOUR back, groping and clawing for traction and footholds on a slippery mountain face.

So how are we going to get started in the right way?? **By strengthening your Inner Framework and talking about ALIGNMENT.** If you want to have a fantastic lifestyle, a ton of money and freedom, and endless choices and opportunity each day, the first thing you need to do is stop being jealous of those people who have it right now. Whaaa?? Moi??? Jealous?? Yep. Whether you're an outright hater or still in the closet about it, you need to address that little green monster. We've all got that guy in us, so let's just have "the talk." Be tough, but non-judgy with this issue. Pause when those feelings of envy surface... that's when I would give you a little nudge and be all, "If you want to be rich, you can't judge the rich." That's a pretty big deal, and has a lot to do with your relationship with money. You want to have money? **You need to respect money!** Years ago I read about a multi-millionaire who was seen picking pennies up off the ground on the sidewalk (I totally wish I knew the book, but I absolutely don't remember... if I did I would give credit here.) Someone asked him why he does that when he's got millions?? He answered to the effect, "Because I respect money, no matter how much **or how little** the amount; I will never walk away from it. When I pick up that penny I say a thank-you to God and tell him that **I'm open to receive more**..." That changed my life and my attitude. From that day on I was picking up pennies off the ground, and adopted the same act of gratitude. If you don't do that now, I think you should start. (How different would the world be if we ALL started to respect and express gratitude for money??) I decided I *wanted* money. I *wanted* that penny. And I ***wanted*** to be open to more! (Plus you just never know when you'll find a good wishing fountain, which I will NEVER pass up!) For the record, 2 things I will not pass up: **Money. Wishes.** You shouldn't either.

Another way I want to work on your Inner Framework is with **John Wooden's Pyramid of Success**. John Wooden was probably about the best College Basketball Coach in the history of forever. From what I can tell, he changed the lives of every single person he came in contact with, and thousands and thousands more that he never even met, like me and you. (He's not alive anymore. But he lived a long great fantastic life.) The Pyramid is just one of the cool life-lessons he came up with for everyone's benefit, but somebody didn't think I should include it in here, since it was such a major part of his work... plus, it's great for him, an old white guy... what I decided to do instead was take the parts I like from HIS Pyramid, and then take what I think are some of the most important aspects of success for the Modern Day, and combine them into my own. So that's what you'll find here. You can and should still Google his work if you've never had much experience with him... he's so inspirational and wise. www.CoachWooden.com

Success is **peace of mind** which is a direct result of

self-satisfaction in knowing you did your best

to become the best that you are capable of being.

- John Wooden,
Head Basketball Coach, Emeritus, UCLA

Success!

Adaptability   Leverage

Relationships   Patience   Love

Reliability   Humor   Poise   Organization

Confidence   Honesty   Communication   Action   Initiative

Discipline   Health   Respect   Faith   Skill   Enthusiasm

DISCIPLINE – There is no substitution for work. Worthwhile results come from hard work and careful planning.

HEALTH – Mental, Moral, Physical, Spiritual, Emotional. Rest + Diet + Exercise = Optimal Energy Levels. Duh! This should not be breaking news for anyone... I mean, really!

RESPECT – Yourself, all those around you, all those depending on you, and Mother Earth. Respect life for the gift that it is and don't be a shit-bag to anyone or anything, including yourself. With respect comes gratitude... and being grateful for all the good things you do have in your world will open you up to receive more.

FAITH – Know that everything works itself out, exactly as it was meant to be. You might be in a learning experience at the moment. In fact if things really suck, you probably are. Have faith that you'll be better and smarter because of all situations.

SKILL – A knowledge of and the ability to properly and quickly execute the fundamentals. Be prepared and always cover every detail as best you can. Be a problem-solver and try to anticipate issues before they occur.

ENTHUSIASM – You must truly enjoy what you are doing, and you will positively influence others with your joy & enthusiasm... people will be better because they came in contact with you.

CONFIDENCE – Respect without fear. When you are thoroughly prepared, you will always feel more confident. When you love and believe in what you do, you will always feel more confident. When you have faith and keep things in the proper perspective with the entire spectrum of your life, you will always feel more confident.

HONESTY – Tell the truth in thought, words, and action. Honesty is the shortest path between 2 points. Problems can be solved when people are honest... they get worse and turn into huge nightmares when people are not.

COMMUNICATION – Proper judgment, respect, and messages to yourself and those around you. Listen sincerely to others. Ask/tell others honestly what you need and expect. Good communication speeds up any transaction and eliminates ridiculousness, which is an energy drain.

ACTION – Determined effort towards clearly defined and noble goals. The

smallest action forward is better than sitting on the couch and watching Bravo TV reruns. The Real Housewives aren't going to make your life any better at all (as entertaining as they are...believe me, I get it... it is fun to watch...)

INITIATIVE – Cultivate the ability to make decisions and think alone when

needed. Do not be afraid of failure, but learn from it. Be able to always move forward on your own accord.

RELIABILITY – Creates respect. When you come thru on what you say, people believe in you.

Expect the same in return, and if you don't get it, communicate the need and the reason behind it.

HUMOR – If you can make people laugh, they will like you. If they like you, they will

begin to trust you. If they like & trust you, and you can make them laugh, people will want to do business with you. Win-Win.

POISE – Being yourself, being at ease in any situation, knowing exactly who you are and

holding your head high because of it, and making peace with your inner demons. Don't fight yourself. Make friends with the real you and everything in life starts to fall into place quicker.

ORGANIZATION – Efficient time and energy management so you get the most

accomplished with the least amount of frustration and redundancy and redundancy and redundancy... see what I'm sayin'??

RELATIONSHIPS – Relationships come from mutual esteem, respect, and beneficial intent at all

times... Don't take these for granted or you'll end up one lonely & bitter mother-effer! These require joint effort and a genuine consideration for others, but OMG! When your relationships are good, all of life is sweeter and more fun. Weeeee!

PATIENCE – Good things take time. They just do. I don't know why and I wish they really didn't

take as long as they usually do... but I'm not in charge of this one at all. Neither are you. Sometimes, you just have to wait on the Universe to give you the "yes."

LOVE – Love yourself. Like 95% of the time when I see myself in the mirror I fall madly in love. The other 5%, well other shit is usually going wrong OR I need some make-up. Still, I'm happy with my ratio, and so should you. **Love others**. Nothing sustainable will happen for you if you hold ill-will for anyone, even your enemies. Before I went to court against this one idiot web-designer whom I'll tell you about a little later, I did weeks of affirmations where I would say "bless" on my inhale and "dude's name" on the exhale. When I saw him in court, it was better. I had let go of a lot of my anger. **Love your friends and family**... love the shit outta them every single second that you can! **Love Earth**. She needs us and gives us so much that we take for granted. **Love life**. The alternative, well I haven't exactly been there myself but I can promise you I'm not ready... so I happily and with a heart filled with gratitude make the most out of every day I'm here! #Truth

ADAPTABILITY – Being able to course correct in any situation and maintain your poise, integrity, and confidence.

LEVERAGE – When your time, energy, productivity, and awesomeness equal far more than the simple sum of adding them together. When you've built relationships and skills and systems that work FOR you, exponentially multiplying your reach, power, scope, message, and financial opportunities. In our modern society, this occurs online.

PLEASE NOTICE THERE IS NO PART OF THE PYRAMID THAT LISTS A COLLEGE DEGREE.

(Not on mine, and not on John Wooden's either if you've Googled his and checked that out.)

Take a look and evaluate where you're at with the Pyramid.... Where are there holes, and how can you fix them? If you say "no holes", I would say you are fabulous, let's meet for drinks, and please pass this on to another person destined for greatness. If there are some holes, that's cool too because we know where to concentrate our efforts. When I first came across John Wooden's Pyramid, working one of my soul-sucking jobs, surfing the internet while pretending to be busy (seriously, that's how I found it), I decided to color in *my* holes with a black Sharpie. Yowza. There they were: my flaws and mistakes along the way in my career, clear as can be, and I wasn't doing so hot... it was evident in my behavior, my lifestyle, my earnings. I just couldn't fake it, looking at it from this point of view. I couldn't pretend there wasn't a problem anymore, and I had to get pretty serious about what I was going to do about it.

It's so cliché, but I decided life really *was* too short (not like the rapper, I mean literally here) and I didn't want to be wandering around with so many black holes anymore. Deep, I know. Cue appropriate and dramatic theme music...

Alright Little-Miss-Sassypants, if you're so against college, why don't you give us some examples of what an 18 year old SHOULD do instead of going to college and making his/her parents proud and securing a good job and future and all that?? Hugh?? Hugh?? What now, hero??

(I'm actually sooooooo glad you asked!)

1. **Travel** – **Europe**, **India**, South America, **China**... check out a world completely different than your own, and notice how your perspective quickly changes when there isn't a McDonalds, 7-11, and Home Depot every other street light. Realize how privileged you truly are! You'll meet other travelers, learn what true poverty is, and get a grasp on what 6000 years of civilization looks like (compared to the 50ish years (max!) that college campus has been standing...). You'll learn survival skills faster than you ever have... and communication skillz too! You might throw up from dysentery... instead of on the frat house bathroom floor. (Gross.) You'll learn that you aren't the center of the Universe, **and that will serve you forever!**

2. **Start a Business.** Intend to make money. Learn **how** to make money. Want so badly to make money that you're excited to wake up every morning and start your day... but don't be surprised if you don't actually make a lot of money. Or even any money. It's the motions and actions you're learning in the beginning, and every life lesson in your own business will make an impact on your future success a million-gazillion times more than case-studies in some lame-ass Economics class. Snoozefest. DO IT FOR REAL! Find mentors, ask to be an intern (without paying college tuition fees to do it), roll your sleeves up, and jump in! Fail! Fail again! F*ck it, fail again and again and again! It's OK! One of these times you will succeed and have learned a TON along the way that will be remembered far longer than a quiz on Probability Ratios and whatever in classes. Whether you succeed or fail, here's what's gonna come out of it all:

You learn how to come up with ideas that will be desired by other people, and you learn to **SELL IT**. You learn to execute and idea, and adapt and change it when needed based on success/failures. You build up an accurate bullshit detector in both yourself & others, **which most definitely does not happen in college.** You meet and socialize with other people on your same mental/creative level... at 18-23 you can harness your alertness/energy to become smarter and greater, or you can kill brain cells at every kegger and tailgate with droves of other kids being duped by the college-gets-you-a-better-job myth of the past. You'll learn adult communication skills at higher levels, and with successes, you might learn to manage and delegate to other people.

3. **Volunteer...** Locally, somewhere else in the US, or Internationally. Go help people less fortunate than you... Make the world better and open your eyes to true poverty and problems on our planet SO THAT YOU CAN LEARN TO BE PART OF THE SOLUTION. This is a life lesson that will serve you 1000x over than textbooks, lecture halls, bong hits, and the munchies.

4. **Pursue and Excel at a Dream You've Always Had...** like hang-gliding. Or surfing. Or zip-lining thru rainforests. Don't just do it once. Study it. Become really excellent at it. Feel those feelings of success after putting your focus on one thing you care about.

5. **Create Things That Have Never Existed Before You.** Get your hands dirty and build something. Create Art. Sculpt. It doesn't matter if you're any good, this is just about being creative and opening yourself up to

the flow of innovation. YOU ARE **NOT** GOING TO BE ENCOURAGED TO INNOVATE IN THE LECTURE HALLS. So take the time now and invent things. Brainstorm. For the first time in your life give yourself permission to truly think for yourself and learn interesting things that make your soul expand. Everything you will ever do in life from this point forward will be better and infused with more creative details if you take the time to cultivate this skill on your own. Write a book, which you'll probably never publish or do anything with because chances are it'll blow. BUT DO IT ANYWAYS because you're developing a voice, an opinion, and confidence at every twist and turn right now. This is a super exciting time when you should literally be living every experience balls out, and I don't mean balls out hammered at 3 am in the frat house... that's a different balls out, and what I'm telling you to avoid right now. Your parents would shit if they knew how you acted in college with their hard earned life savings to get you there under the guise of "higher education."

6. Master a Sport. Don't just learn it or try it or do it, I mean MASTER IT.

Become the absolute best you can possibly be at just one thing for now. You'll be afraid to fail, and you'll move through it. You'll get frustrated and want to quit, but you'll conquer those feelings. You'll feel the guilt of procrastination, and become dedicated enough to turn that into focused action. And you'll get in better physical shape... increase your metabolism, muscle tone & flexibility... probably start to eat better... reduce stress levels and find a new dimension of confidence and inner peace... meet new and different people who share the same interest as you... and most likely carry these new habits through the rest of your life. Holla!

It makes me elated to point out that in today's NEW economy and job market, if you were to apply for a job with a college degree, you would fall into the stacks and stacks of other qualified college-degreed candidates, under-employed candidates, and former-employees-who-used-to-work-there-and-got-laid-off candidates. I'd bet you a cocktail you'll never hear from them again, but you probably have no money so I'd have to buy even if I won. But, if in lieu of a college degree you were able to say that you had spent a year in Europe and now speak several languages as well as having created an entire network of professional contacts over there, had been building schools and equipping teachers to educate children in South America, or studied Ancient Eastern Philosophy and Martial Arts in China... well, now you're a rockstar! You're interesting, unique, different, and real! You've just become so different from everyone else, and you will be remembered. You'll most likely get called back, at least for the interview. (I've got a whole list of Questions/Answers to help you thru any Interview on my website www.SonjaLandis.com)

While in Europe, South America, and China did you party and have an amazing time?? Hellz yeah, I sure hope so! That's the freedom, energy and excitement of young adulthood... and it's best cultivated in a natural environment where you can also build life skills, rather than creating enormous debt almost zero real-world experience on a somewhat isolated college campus. I'm telling you to run with the young adult time in your life and make it as amazing as possible! You don't have to pay thousands of dollars per credit hour and read a book about life... you should actually go live yours instead!

go find yourself

Businesses and Corporations today are waking up to the fact that we are a global economy and business is now done worldwide, online, and thru Social Media and relationships. None of that equates to a college degree, but your real-life skills, confidence, and network does! And here's the thing: if anyone is going to hold NOT having a college degree against you, I promise you, you don't want to work there anyways! They aren't progressive enough, and they're probably suffering financially because of it. You don't want that job. You want to be with the movers and shakers, the change agents, the creative problem-solvers. You are here to make a difference. So go do that!

:: Fundamental ::

- serving as an original or generating source; a basis supporting existence or determining **essential structure**

- structure, function, facts, or **general principles** and governing truths

- the **lowest component of a complex event** or situation

- **of central importance**

- belonging to one's innate or **ingrained characteristics** : DEEP-ROOTED

A perfect illustration of the importance of fundamentals:

National Lampoon's Vacation. One of the best cult-classic comedies everrrrrr. Chevy Chase ala Clark Griswold about to take his beloved family across country to Wally World. New station wagon for the adventure ("You think you hate it now, but wait till you drive it."), check. Luggage, check. Ability to back out of the garage with said luggage mounted above said station wagon, whoopsies. You can't get all the way to Wally World if you can't get out of the garage. Look again at those aspects of the definition above. Fundamentals are of central importance. They'll get you out of the garage and on your way...

Wally World is your ideal lifestyle, where you feel fulfilled and inspired in your career with

time and balance to spend nurturing your family, friends, relationships, and passions/hobbies. You're engaged (not exhausted), eager (not overwhelmed), and fully awake (not just going thru the motions). The station wagon is the way in which you're going to get your message, your products, your services, and your career out into the world. The luggage is all of your unique attributes, personality, gifts, ideas, knowledge, products, services, and business you provide in that Wally World ideal lifestyle... You're on your way! Until you can't get out of the garage, and the luggage gets all effed up and discombobulated and you have to repack everything because you didn't get the fundamentals right... this book teaches fundamental skills for the changing Modern times and New Economy, and it also provides a good map for you to follow (so you don't end up in the wrong hood in St. Louis at night, paying for directions and having your rims stolen).

TRADITIONAL, OLD SCHOOL, TRIED & TRUE SKILLS THAT ENDURE

ORGANIZATION

If you're going to make changes in your life and move towards who you are really meant to become, you're gonna be hella busy. Busier than you've ever been, but completely juiced with an energy known as *passion*, which is saaa-weeeet. One of the most important ways to conserve time and energy is to start and stay organized, which is easier said than done. (As a Businesswoman AND an Artist, this was extremely challenging... but if you're super creative like me, look at it as the ying and yang, and that they are equally important. Get a journal or notebook to write down every important detail, phone number, and idea **in one place**. You're going to be setting up websites and a strategic online presence, and you'll have more passwords than you ever imagined possible. It is imperative to keep these in one spot or you will get frustrated and inefficient... two things you **don't** need in life!

 Get a bunch of those 15¢ colored paper folders and label them with aspects of what you want to do. If you're a writer, you can make each folder a Chapter and start to organize your topics, resources, and ideas.

 Keep your receipts and write everything off on your taxes, **which also sends a powerful message to your own subconscious and the Universe that you are serious about this.**

If you can set up a little office, do that. If you can't, keep everything in a laundry basket that you can slide away when needed and grab back out quickly when it's time to work. Get some simple office supplies you'll need and keep them in the basket (**don't** let anyone in the house use them cuz they'll be lost and you'll spend time looking for that stapler "you could've sworn you saw right here!!!" and that's inefficient).

Set up a new email account to use just for your business stuff, and once things start rolling, divide what comes into the inbox into subfolders (either by people's names, or invoices, press and media contacts, passwords, urgent, etc...). ANYTHING you can do to get organized, do it. You'll save yourself a ton of time and hassle, and you'll start off on the right foot.

AUTHENTICITY

:: Authenticity ::

Refers to the truthfulness of origins, attributions, commitments, sincerity, devotion, and intentions... A philosophy, or particular and expressive way of dealing with the world, being faithful to internal rather than external ideas.

Authenticity is being real, like the Velveteen Rabbit. Once you're real, don't let anyone make you unreal again. **Stay your path, listen to your intuition, and make a commitment to yourself to be better each day.**

Authenticity = Alignment = Awake = Alive

PRINCIPLES – ETHICS – VALUES

I want to do **good**. I want the world

to be **better** because **I** was here.

-Will Smith

Do everything with excellence, the intention to make the world and other people's lives better, and honesty, and you'll always do well. Have the **best of intentions** for yourself, your family, your ideal clients, and your work. It's really difficult to always do the most ethical thing when you want so bad to cut corners or take short-cuts, and you're desperate to **succeed**. From my experience, every "short-cut" ended up leading to a string of bad decisions, and got me farther from where I intended to be. Take every opportunity that makes sense, but not necessarily every "short-cut," and you'll know the difference in your gut. If it feels slimy, and you wouldn't want it done to you/your child/your mom, **and you wouldn't want others to find out about it**... then it's a bad choice, no matter what the possible outcome "could" be. If you "could" make a ton of money, but it has the twinge of any of the aforementioned red-flags, it's not worth it. The outcome will be tainted, your karma will be yucky, and it won't get you truly closer to who you want to be. The slower and more solid way of building your dreams, lifestyle, and business, based on principles, ethics, values, and a sense of service to the planet will be abundantly rewarding in every way. Make the world better, make people happier, smarter, or more confident than before they met you, and you'll have wealth flowing your way in no time! (Trust me!)

PERSPECTIVE

www.weblamers.com

We see the world, not as *it is*,

but as **we are** – or, as we are **conditioned** to see it.

- Stephen Covey

The 7 Habits of Highly Effective People

Everything you see and feel affects your behaviors, your actions, and eventually your outcomes. The important thing is to keep in mind it's only from *your own perspective*, and everyone else has their perspective too. Sometimes those perspectives are close and seem to match, and sometimes they don't. One of the key concepts of business, relationships, and life in general is to stay true to your own barometer and direction, while realizing everyone else around you has the right to their perspective... and their perspective is affecting their views, feelings, behaviors, actions and outcomes. The more you try to understand and acknowledge another's perspective, especially your ideal clients in business, the more successful you'll be. Their perspective is also their TRUTH, and relating/understanding to it is a far more **effective strategy** than to try and convince anyone that **your** perspective is right. It doesn't work, and it's a waste of your energy. Instead, always try to get to the root of one's perspective (views, feelings, behaviors, actions, outcomes), whether it be your OWN or someone else's.

DISCIPLINE

I merely took the energy it takes to pout

and wrote some blues.

- Duke Ellington

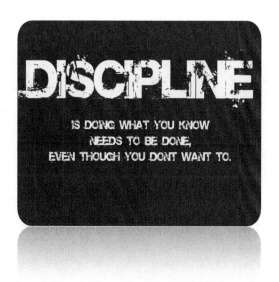

Michael Jordan. Michael Jordan <u>missed</u> more than 9000 game shots, and untold amounts, probably tens of thousands, in practice. He was the first person on the court, and the last person to leave. He played injured. He played sick. He played after his father was murdered. And that amount of discipline made him the best in the world, changing the game of basketball, the Nike brand, and the sports world forever.

Geez, those are some big Air Jordans to fill, and I'm certainly not the chick to do it. (Besides, I like my Jimmy Choos, thank you very much.) MJ has more discipline in his little finger than I have, and I have more than most! The point is this: you won't get very far without a little discipline. It's easier to be disciplined doing what you love, not doing some shit for someone else. If there's going to be hard work, long hours, stress, headache, and heartache involved, I want it to be for my own business and my own life and my own family's benefit and my own dreams/goals, not someone else's!

No matter what, you've got to have a degree of discipline to function as an adult in our society, otherwise you wouldn't set the alarm clock and get your ass in the car to drive to work in the mornings. If you follow the principles and action steps I've got outlined for you in this book and apply some discipline, you could get to the point where it's all for YOU and YOUR DREAM CAREER instead of whatever soul-sucking job you're doing now. (I totally feel your pain... I was in the soul-sucking arena for a long time myself!)

Why is "patience" a virtue? Why can't "hurry the fuck up" be a virtue?

your ⓔ cards
someecards.com

© www.SomeECards.com

As for me, I work from home now. I had my own Art Gallery, which **I'd now like to present as one of my most colossal and expensive flops ever:** I wanted my own Gallery for about 12 years, and when I *finally* got it, I hated it. It was a ton of work, constant headaches and issues, and took up every single bit of my time and energy. My landlords were of zero help, which was so sad because the property was effing phenomenal, just steps from the Pacific Ocean and in one of the coolest areas on San Diego, the Cedros Design District. (I would totally check it if you're ever in the area!) The 20ish minute commute didn't seem bad at first, but started to wear on me... not to mention it easily extended to 35-40 mins with traffic. I had a crazy nut-case who would come into my Gallery and ask me the exact same questions, tell me the exact same family stories, then ask me out every single day. No joke. Every. Single. Day. (According to "Crazy Johnny" as I refer to him, he was apparently "14th Generation Solana Beach", which is quite a feat, basically, like, his family had settled the area back in the Caveman days.) The energy of the place was bad, which I know sounds like some hoo-ey New Age bullshit, but the truth is I'm an Artist and I'm sensitive to stuff like that. I assure it's not hoo-ey. The absolute deal breaker: a leaky roof, which ruined some of my canvases. After 60 days and several *ignored* written requests to the landlords to please fix that roof (and the dry rotted front deck which was a $1million lawsuit waiting to happen), I had enough. I cried and was bummed, and then I broke my lease and moved out of my Gallery. I **QUICKLY** and **MOST DEFINITELY** realized I wanted to work/paint/write from home, where I could also nest and take care of my family and be close to my son's school. I have to say, the commute from my bedroom to the office isn't bad these days! My boss, she's pretty rad too, BTW. (BTW = by the way, if you're not down with the text lingo these days)

Can I tell you what happened right after I made the decision to break the lease and lose out on the months and months of blood, sweat, and tears I put into my Gallery?? I got connected with Crayola, who loves The Painted Laugh and wanted to promote me on their Facebook page, amongst other projects we've got in the works. I was asked to become a permanent exhibit in a new Children's Art Museum in Florida opening in 2013, where I figured out I could pursue MORE Children's Art Museums across the country, getting my Art out there without any overhead costs, rent, utilities, or Crazy Johnny. I got inspired to write this book. I got sponsored for ArtPrize in Grand Rapids, Michigan... which is a ground-breaking kind of Art Contest and Festival that takes over 3 square miles in the city for several weeks. It's kick-ass, to say the least. I also got a sweet venue as the sponsor, which doesn't hurt! And lastly I was invited to submit a presentation for The Art Institute of Chicago's upcoming "Sound As Art Symposium"... none of which would have been possible had I decided to keep pouring my energy into that Gallery, which wasn't working out.

There are some valuable lessons learned with that expensive and time consuming nightmare I went thru: I didn't check into the past of that property, mostly because I was emotionally connected to it. I had fallen in love with that spot, and I ignored a lot of red flags and didn't do a proper walk-thru on the property before signing the lease. Had I talked to some of the other business owners first, I would have also found out these landlords are notorious for being difficult to work with and refusing to improve/repair their property. I also, and most importantly, re-learned in the most obvious way that when one door closes, another one (or a few) open. I'm glad it happened, because now I don't have that want inside me anymore for a physical Gallery location, and if I hadn't gone for it, I wouldn't know better. I also have a better grasp of how much easier and better business really runs online, and there's tremendous power, leverage, and profits in that!

I wanted to take a minute and introduce you to my brother, Nick. If you're a single girl, he's also very cute. Proof:

© Jim Henson, I imagine, on that "Animal" one

He chose to pursue a career based on his passion, and he's got a little bit to say on the discipline it takes to make it all happen. He runs a Spring Break Tour Company for college students ventures to Mexico, which became a tough sell over the past couple years with the economy and the drug wars/bad press in our south-of-the-border neighbor these days... Sad. Really heartbreaking to my brother, who developed this deep love and passion for not only tourism, travel, and the exploration of other cultures (he actually travels all over Europe as well), but for the Mexican people who build their livelihoods on our American tourism. He started an entire campaign for the media to tell the true stories and paint a better picture of Mexico and its people called SpeakWellAca. (Acapulco)

He pretty much throws parties and events, *as his "job."* Yes, for reals. He's going to talk about Discipline here, but he's also very good at leveraging his efforts: from his Spring Break Tours he's opened a Young Adult Travel Division specializing in trips to Playa Del Carmen for the January International Electro Music Festival and Las Vegas, well, for Vegas. He is one of the top New Year's Eve Event Promoters for Chicago, trafficking more than 3,000 party people at each sold-out venue for the night. He also takes a cut for the electronic sales for all of his events, becoming an **Affiliate** (which we'll talk about again later) with companies such as Neptix and Groupon-type companies. So without further ado, my brother Nick:

"

I am my own boss. I'm an Independent Contractor, Entrepreneur, Self-Employed Company of 1. I

had a ton to say, but my big sister told me to "write my OWN book" and that I had to cut it down... (typical!) So I had to shrink this excerpt down like my hairline... too bad it wasn't my waistline! Ugh,

getting older is hard!!! So here goes, my take on **DISCIPLINE**: I work extremely hard to architect events and travel packages with my customers' best interests always in mind as the corner-stone for everything I touch. I will sacrifice cost, expenses, and personal time on my end to deliver what is most favorable for my audience... which leads to client loyalty & retention... and profits! I knew from an early age and quite simply, I wanted to make a difference for people, be influential, and put smiles on other's faces. **My work felt done when I made others feel good.** I'm hooked on the vibrancy, the never-ending "Thank Yous!," and the lifelong memories I get to create for people. Success takes discipline though, and this works for me:

1. **LOOK THE PART.** Look like a professional and mirror the attitude/message you wish to portray. Do I exchange $1000 Prada shades and Swim Trunks for the grey Calvin Klein 3-piece suit?? Yep. It's still a write-off come tax time! Keep yourself looking and feeling as good and healthy as possible, and that takes a strong level of discipline. Eat right, exercise, drink in moderation, stay professional. These practices, along with a steady supply of Rogaine are what keep me on track to **LOOK THE PART** I need to for my career.

2. **ACT THE PART.** *I can be anyone I want to be at any given time.* I have the ability (and I suggest you try this too) to play a character in your business world. I mean after all, our work shouldn't define us as the people we are, but rather, a means to earn a living & lifestyle for the people we want to be. Far too often, we let careers define us as people, when it should be the other way around! *My career allows me to be who I am and live how I desire!* I can be anyone I need to be at any given time and place. I can control the situation and switch roles faster than some ex-girlfriends with multiple personality disorder. (NOT any of mine, of course... just sayin') Example: The way I speak to some of the most popular, world-renowned (and sometimes diva-like) DJs in trying to book their talent is far different than the way I speak to concerned parents sending their son/daughter college kid on an International trip of my design. It's not as if your customers/clients aren't getting the "real you;" it's just that they are getting the **BEST PART OF YOU** for that situation. Have the discipline to act calm in heated situations, and separate <u>who</u> you are from the emotionality of your work.

3. **BE THE PART**. You better know your stuff, and be the expert of your career field! You must be self-disciplined to practice personal development to stay on top of your game... After all, there are no MANDATORY COMPANY conferences and seminars that your "boss" is forcing you to attend. I'm forced to be my own toughest critic. I study and learn other languages, read about global issues, attend travel conventions, and research all events and productions I take on.

When you love what you're doing, it almost doesn't even feel like work at all. This is what I'd want to do anyway, because it's what I truly LOVE. It's important to focus on what you do well and say "no, thanks" when you must; this is to benefit your career AND personal sanity. Don't take on too much or you'll run out of hours in the day, grind yourself down, and lose focus on what you specialize in. It takes DISCIPLINE to stay

"

knowledgeable, self-evaluate, and work HARD (and a lot of odd hours!).

POSITIVE ATTITUDE OF SUCCESS

Well I guess for right now, while you're reading this book, it *is* my job a little bit... but only until you're soooo ready to take on the world and have the strength and courage to do it on your own, ok?!?! I have plenty of attitude to lend you! I'm not talking that snarky, sarcastic attitude I throw around so haphazardly either. I'm talking about an attitude where you **expect great things to happen to you** because YOU are putting great things into the world... where you **expect people to be**

honest and truthful and exceed because YOU are honest and truthful and exceeding in what you do. It's the attitude of greatness, of being fulfilled and truly happy and grateful for all the things you have in your life, and of genuine enthusiasm for what you do in your waking hours. (Most of that directly ties to, you guessed it, your career path...!) It's the attitude that YOU WILL, WITHOUT A SHADOW OF A DOUBT, EVENTUALLY SUCCEED AT WHATEVER YOU PUT YOUR MIND TO. Note the "eventually" in there... and that is ooohh to the kizay! We'll be addressing that all throughout the book: the flops, missteps, and whoopsies that are all part of any learning process. I've made many of them for you, and I will be pointing them out in no particular order of disasters all along this tour, hopefully saving you some trouble on your own path!

You gotta start somewhere, sister. ("Sister" of course meaning my guys out there too... just go with it.) It might as well be in your own house. Try this: Grab a Sharpie and Post-Its or whatever. Write down 5 words about how you want to FEEL everyday of your life, then with a smaller pen, write down adjectives that describe how that *feels to you*. Nobody's will be the same, it's just how you define it to you. Now put those Post-Its up on your mirror where you destroy your hair everyday with the flatiron. That's where mine are! At first, I felt like an asshole doing this and I would take them down if people were coming over because it felt both very personal and dorky. **I felt like a big nerd.** Then I realized: I was trying to "hide" those things that I wanted to remind myself to radiate into the world. Duh. How could I hide it and radiate it at the same time?? Doesn't make sense... goes right along with my semi-genius scheme in College of taking what I *really* wanted to do in life (be an Artist) and hide it away where it was safe. Once I figured out this was another way of being afraid to expose myself, be vulnerable and possibly fail, I happily left them up there, letting my Freak Flag fly! Peeps could think it was weird if they wanted (which they don't, they might do the same thing on their own mirror).

So here are mine in alphabetical order:

ACCOMPLISHED

Recognized – Important – Popular – Attracting Positive Media Attention

AFFLUENT

Wealthy – Generous to Others – Free – A Life Full of Options & Choices – Secure – Great Stuff I Like – Travel

CREATIVE

Artistic – Abundant With Ideas – Influential – Inspired – Inspiring – Funny – Aligned

GENEROUS

Wealthy – Friendly – Helpful – Compassionate – Kind – Smiling

LOVING

Affectionate – Playful – Fun – Funny – Relaxed – Peaceful – Healthy – Friendly

Those things are what get me to walk around my house like a fucking champion! Those are the qualities I want to radiate and feelings I want to feel every day, in every way possible, whether it be with my career, my parenting style, my relationships with others, my love life, the person at the stoplight waiting to cross, the drivers next to me with all their pent-up road-rage, etc... Alright, all-star, time to pick your own, and time to focus your attitude in that direction!

TIME MANAGEMENT

Honestly, you have time! You have more time than you realize... but you need to turn off the TV. I enjoy shit-shows as much as anyone else, but it literally sucks and drains your life force like a vampire. TV is an escape, and peeps totally zone out from their sucky life into the tube and internet... that effing facebook is the most addictive, time-wasting, AMAZINGLY USEFUL AT TIMES, invention ever. (So far. Now Google+ is coming along, possibly a one-upper... Good Lord!) No sugar coating this: you have to trade time **now** for freedom of lifestyle, health, and happiness **down the road**. Turn off the TV. Make the choice to start creating an amazing life instead of <u>watching</u> people lead amazing lives. Or Snooki.

Don't say you don't have enough time.

YOU have **exactly the same number of hours per day** that were given to Helen Keller, Michelangelo, Mother Teresa, Leonardo da Vinci, Thomas Jefferson, Albert Einstein, and the Wright Brothers.

YOU have **exactly the same amount of time in your day** as Lance Armstrong, Lady Gaga, and Oprah.

You have exactly the same amount of time as me.

You have the time. This is your life we're talking about.

THE KEY TO LIFE IS VERY SIMPLE:

Find what makes you happy.

Find who makes you happy.

Spend your time doing those things with those people.

Realize what makes you miserable.

Realize who makes you miserable.

Avoid those situations and people in every way possible.

RELATIONSHIPS

Don't be an island. It's lonely, it's ineffective, and it's waaaaaaayyy more work. All of which add to more stress than should be required. There are a couple relationships to cultivate here: Professional and Personal. Bottom line, it's GOT to be Win-Win. Period. The dynamic you set up in the beginning will always stick and linger... if it's Win-Win and equal from the start, you will build trust, rapport, and a strong bond. If it's off balance, and one person provides more, one person demands more, one person carries the load more, one person acts like the parent and one like the child, it will be the underlying dynamic in that relationship forever, no matter what changes. **Trust me.** Make it a balanced, Win-Win situation from the start if you want to maintain any relationships long-term!

- PROFESSIONAL
  - Affiliates
    - An Affiliate is another person or company or product, usually with a website, that correlates with you and your message/product/idea, and when partnered together and talking positively about one another, benefits you both. Often times an Affiliate will share in part of the profits of clients/sales they send your direction, and you'll get part of the profits of clients/sales you send their way. Win-Win.
  - Bloggers
    - Ohhhhh, the power of the Mommy/Daddy/"Green" (Environmental) Bloggers! They're relatable, transparent, and influential beyond belief. **Befriend the Bloggers!**
  - Corporate Sponsors
    - When you get this, you've literally just moved into the fast lane. It's not going to happen without a very big **WIN** for them, which ends up being a big WIN for you! They need to see their own **WIN** first, and they need to see it very clearly.
  - Non-Profit Organizations
    - An awesome relationship to build, and if you cultivate this relationship right, you're going to be of service far bigger than yourself and anything you ever thought, and that is a seriously abundant lifestyle to lead.

- PERSONAL
  - Your Support System
    - Keep constructive people in your life, and protect your dreams/ideas while they're fresh and new... it's a vulnerable time, and you need to be a warrior right now. **Protect your vision from getting squashed!**
  - You, Yourself, and You – A Love Story
    - Let's finally start saying nice, helpful things to ourselves.
    - Read Shel Silverstein's *The Missing Piece Meets the Big O* – it's a kid's book with the BEST relationship advice you will ever read. And it'll take you all of, like, 7.3 minutes.

KEEP **AWAY** from people who try to belittle your ambitions.

Small people always do that, but the **really great** make you feel that you, too, can

become great.

-Mark Twain

A SNIPPET FROM MY LIFE ABOUT RELATIONSHIPS:

I instantly befriend South Africans with this little ice-breaker – always a hit* and lots of fun. It's yours for the taking, if you wish. No credit necessary as this is common Google knowledge. I happened to get it straight from my South African neighbor's mouth one night at a Halloween Party, and I've been using it ever since. Plus, you'll stun people if it's ever a Jeopardy or Trivial Pursuit question. (Good God in Heaven, does anyone still play that?!?!)

*Note: **NOT** ALWAYS a hit… People from West Africa, or ANY PART OF AFRICA besides South Africa, or whose parents are from South Africa but they didn't *actually* grow up or spend time there will look at you just like any/every Midwest Iowa Farmer when trying to bond with this fun fact: like your batshit crazy. Indeed.

How to Become Friends with, or maybe just do shots with, South African Strangers

Don't try this with Brits or Australians, whose accent is similar to an untrained ear like mine… wait for a clear sign of being from South Africa, like actually hearing, "In South Africa…" or "Growing up in South Africa," or if the World Cup is on and they are **without a doubt** supporting South Africa, it's a GO.

Say to them, "Ahhhh, you're from South Africa! I know a GREAT thing about South Africa, one of my favorite things! I know about the Amarula (ahm-uh-roo-luh) Fruit*, and how all the jungle animals come and get drunk together!" If you're at a bar, pub, or party where you/the South Africans/preferably both have already knocked one or two back, you're instant friends. In my experience you will be bought shots… (which never works out because I can't do shots. It's an unfortunate quick to puke/easily blacks out combo I have, so I just stay away… Any good South African worth his salt will gladly down that shot he just bought for you, no problems.) Here's where I will deviate: if it happens to be an actual Amarula Shot... The Amarula Liqueur **tastes good** and is fairly weak in proof, plus it's the novelty of it all, and I'm pretty sure your **new** South African friends *might* be offended if I/you turned it down... Just to be sure, I've never refused it.

*Amarula Fruit grows super high up in the trees in South Africa, I think the story is tall, skinny, slippery trees that are too difficult for even the cheekiest little monkey to climb. Once a year though, the fruit ripens and falls off the trees to the ground, and in the hot sun quickly ferments into Amarala Liqueur. All the jungle animals are down and ready to paaarrrr-taaayyy! They all instinctively know this timing of events, and band together for the time being, setting whatever differences aside, and go get hammered together. Really. Google it, and you'll see videos of prairie dogs and wild boars, monkeys and elephants all staggering around, head butting trees, passing out on top of each other in a big heap. How fun is that?? Don't say I never taught you anything! Oh, I'm pretty sure they still don't invite the lions or big cats... clearly some animals cannot be trusted on the sauce.

Alcohol certainly need not be initially involved for this relationship building activity with South African people. I've even tried it with a famous South African Rock Star the first time I met her, and we instantly and soberly bonded. (Although she did say she had a bottle of Amarula Fruit Liqueur at home that we need to split sometime. Man, South Africans are soooo bomb.) Anyway, my friend Esjay Jones is about 6 foot 2 and oozes moxie-rockstar. She walks in the room, **and owns it**. She performs on stage, **and owns it**. You should Google her or find her on iTunes or whatever.

Her voice is sultry, her guitar is gangsta, and her style is punk rock. Her vocals are sometimes rated R and beyond, as any good Rock Star's should be. She speaks right to your soul, so I think you'll really dig her music. Thank me later.

COMMUNICATION

Use a person's first name. It's a compliment, and everyone likes to hear their own name being said. Don't over-use it! That would be weird and on the verge of creepy. (People DON'T like that! Ick.)

So the basics are we communicate with verbals and non-verbals, tone, body language, eye-contact, words, expressions, posture, and personal space... we communicate respect and interest when we talk AND when we listen and respond accordingly. I mean, as much as you can, pay attention to how you're communicating with the world, and as for me I always try to be cucumber cool. I don't road rage (it's bad for my complexion), even when someone cuts me off. (*Dude/Chick cuts me off. I slam on brakes. OK, that sucked. Instead of getting pissed-off like I kinda used to do, I'm instead thankful I didn't have an accident, which would slow me down a lot more than getting cut off.)* We all need to do our best with both communication AND road rage, and that's not easy.

Poor communication leads to bad attitudes, resentment, and burned bridges, and none of that seemed to me like the road to lollipops and gumdrops that I wanted. Have I ever absolutely lost my shit? Yeah, dude. I'm divorced. Duh. *(I've had moments with my head on full-swivel, Poltergeist style... then afterwards I'm all, geez... that wasn't very cool of me. Note to self: do better.)* But I have tried to analyze my OWN flaws and communication barriers, and **I work on it all the time**. It's not easy! I'm super-duper non-confrontational, and at times, I've gotten myself into a world of suck because I didn't communicate my thoughts and feelings about situations well. My advice is to take responsibility for about **half** of every situation, good and bad. Give yourself credit when it's due and accept some blame for the stinkies. Besides that, just be mindful, respectful, assertive, and kind. It's sometimes easy, sometimes hard, and always a little bit of effort. Like everything else in life!

(P.S. Don't road rage on me or anyone else, either, man. We all make mistakes. You eff up too, so just freakin' relax, yo, and take your Xanax!)

((P.S.S. I wrote another little sumthin' sumthin' on communication you might want to check out. It's called: **Cordial Communication** *A Quick & Hilarious Guide to Conversations with People You'd Rather Punch* and it's available on my website www.SonjaLandis.com at the time of this book going into print... I might put *Cordial Communication Guide* up on Amazon, too, but haven't decided yet.))

MODERN, NEW SCHOOL SKILLS, WELCOME TO 2011, JUMP ON!

LEVERAGE

I am only one, **BUT I AM ONE.**

I cannot do everything, **but I can do something.**

And I will not let what I cannot do interfere with what I can do.

- Edward Everett Hale

That quote from Edward Everett Hale is absolutely true. Good ideas, change, and invention starts with just one person. But welcome to 2011... where you can quickly and easily unite a whole lotta those "ones" to create an immense force of effective power. "One" can quickly become a "tribe." (read Seth Godin!) Tribes can and do change the world. Leaders of tribes, or unique and passionate people positioned within tribes, can not only positively change the world but make a ton of money doing it. People making a ton of money, doing what they love, getting to lead the amazing lifestyle they deserve AND who continue to influence more positive change and Charity/Foundation/Research work. That's leverage. That's how it's done. And in our modern society, it's done online and with Mobile Marketing, Social Media, and YouTube.

There's this truly fascinating, smart, wonderful chick I know named **Tammi DeVille**. She is so sweet and kind she probably never has cussed one swear word in her life. (Because she *is* so great and giving, I somehow talked her into contributing to *my* totally scandalous book not even 18 inches from your nose!) She is leading a tribe of people and wrote an inspirational, life-changing book about the power of Community Service and Volunteer Work. That's the power that can happen when one person affects many. It creates leverage, and we're going to talk about how to do that for you, too. Here's Tammi's book. You should really check it out and start to brainstorm how you're going to change the world for the better...

www.onatuesdaynight.com

http://www.cafepress.com/onatuesdaynight

facebook: Changing The World on a Tuesday Night

Maybe we can start a revolution.

Maybe we can start on Tuesday.

Maybe, if we work together and each pitch in just a couple of hours a week,

we can feed all the hungry, advocate for all the animals, support every kid's dream.

I wrote a book about ordinary people making an extraordinary difference.

The book is about **you** being one of them.

- Tammi DeVille

TRANSPERENCY

www.five-words.tumblr.com

And while you're being who you want to be, be very **honest** and respectful of people. That's called transperency. Letting people see into your world. Letting them see the bads that led up to the goods. Let them see you be genuine and real. Tell people what works/worked for you as well what doesn't/didn't. People's BS meters are verrryyy high these days, and you can almost hear a person's sphincter tighten up when you're trying to get one over on them... They're not gonna appreciate it, and they're not gonna forget it.

(This is one of the reasons I was so bad at those other jobs I tried to do... Not only did I have zero passion for those j-o-b-s, I actually had a repulsion for them... which came across, as it should, as disingenuous BS, sometimes to others, but mostly to MYSELF.) The worst thing you can do is try to lie to yourself. It absolutely does not work. **You will always know the truth.**

Tell the truth. Tell the truth. Tell the truth.

All the time.

- Randy Pausch
The Last Lecture

Especially and most importantly tell the truth to yourself! If you're not honest with yourself, it becomes a snowball effect of lies on a lot of other people in the world. Some people will try to convince you to lie to yourself in the first place, when you know better. They might do it because they believe they're looking out for you; they might be trying to make you fit into their truth instead of your own. Either way, it's just. not. going. to. work. PLUS, it's way better to tell YOUR OWN truth from the get-go. Sometimes you don't know for sure it's a lie, and I get that completely. Deeeeeeeeeeeeeep down, I think you do. (I did.) Usually we'll suppress that intuitive thought until it manifests itself, say in the form of a fun stress-induced kidney stone/anxiety attack combo when you're only 30 years old.

Life is short, and this is it. This is the youngest you're ever going to be, right now. Boom. Another second went by, and you're older. Another. Another. Get the idea?? You are NOT Benjamin Button, and there is no better time than to start telling the true story of your very own life, passion, and phenomenal ideas than RIGHT NOW. I know it's hard to do, but I also know it's both possible and worth it!

ONLINE PRESENCE – BLOG – HEADSHOTS – STAGING

I CAN BE GOOGLED, THEREFORE I AM.

www.google.com of course!

NO MATTER WHAT YOUR BUSINESS IS, you're going to need a website, because it's 2011 and things are never ever ever ever going to move backward toward "good ole days" type of business. If you're not online, you're going to be left in the dust in several ways. I've got the process broken down for you in Chapter 12, and that's just how you do it: step-by-step. **It feels overwhelming at first**, but I'm going to show you the Road and the Map, so don't you fret and flounder about it!

You're going to set up a blog, which you can think of as nothing more than extended Facebook statuses, really. You'll probably end up saying a little bit more than a status, but you don't have to. Your blog is going to be part of the website, and it'll happen step-by-step too.

You're going to need to take a nice picture of yourself, or a "headshot." Like a model. This is a picture of just you **by yourself**, not one where you crop out the person next to you. This is a picture you can take yourself *if your camera has a timer*, but you will **NOT** be holding the camera in front of yourself or taking a picture in the mirror. IF YOU HAVE ANY OF THESE, DON'T USE THEM ON YOUR PROFESSIONAL WEBSITES OR PAGES. Stay away from patterns and cheesy poses. Be natural. Simple. Professional. Modern.

We're going to talk a lot about the importance of "Positioning" in the book, and part of that is the staging and background of those headshots. It's so simple: just pick a plain background, and a plain color shirt/blouse that you feel looks great on you. Pinks, blues, and purples are all good. I love black and wear it a lot, but it's a color that comes across as "un-relatable" to some people. If wearing black is your thing, however, wear it! (As an Artist I usually wear blacks, silvers, and grays so as not to detract from my Art that I want to take Center Stage.) The big deal here, above all, is a professional image. Make sure the kitty-litter box, or the dog's toys, or the kid's toys, or the laundry isn't in the background. Don't take the picture in your bathroom with "the throne" in any mirror reflections. Matter of fact, let's stay away from the bathroom and pictures all together, just to be safe. Please. You can play around on a website called www.picnik.com for FREE and do enough photo-editing to make it look like a photographer took it, and you can pay $5/month for even more functions (but that's not really necessary). Until you want to drop some coin on a professional photo shoot (which is usually worth it and something you will probably want to **eventually** do!!!), then following these simple rules and doing a bit of "picnik" on it will be just fine.

© www.SomeECards.com

POSITIONING

We're going to talk more about positioning yourself as an expert throughout this book, but one of the essential things we need to start with is **YOUR perception of your position**. (I had this issue too, big time!) I'm a talented Artist, and I love what I do... but I hadn't gone to "school" for it, therefore I had a hard time giving *myself* permission to be good, talented, and abundant for doing what I loved, what I really wanted to do. It also feels weird (at first) to charge a price for what comes easy to you, natural to you, and happily to you... our society has gotten so sadly conditioned that the majority of people equate money with hard, shitty work. That's soooo not good. At. All! We're going to talk about **HOW** to position yourself later, but first you need to **give yourself that permission** and **claim expert status for what you love.** You're the expert if you say you are, and focus on being amazing at it. No lie... if you go balls out to claim that expert status, no one (but the occasional jealous haters) will argue with it. (And if there are **no** haters, you're not up to much. Which is exactly why we're here – to get you up to some great stuff ASAP.)

P.S. Not going to school for something equates to both self-taught and naturally bad-ass talented, so claim that and **be proud**. Word.

CREATIVITY

Don't just GO with the **flow**. Realize that YOU **ARE** the **flow.**

Creativity is the juice and spark **that gives everything in your life**: your ideas, your communication, your marketing, your potential, your passion, your business, your relationships... **vitality and innovation.**

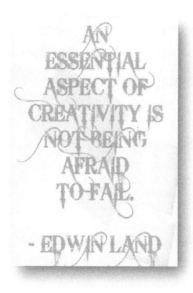

AN ESSENTIAL ASPECT OF CREATIVITY IS NOT BEING AFRAID TO FAIL.

- EDWIN LAND

Please don't say anything about "not being creative". Everyone is creative. Humans, by design, are creative. If you weren't meant to be creative, you wouldn't have been given the gift of the most-highly evolved brain and the ever-popular opposable thumbs. If you feel like you're not in a very creative state, it's because you've taken away your own permission to be it. Good news is, you can give yourself the permission back, too! You're *really* in charge here, so if you've got a complaint, there's only **one person** to address where it'll make the difference. (That's YOU, dollface.)

Be kind but firm with yourself when you decide to get the permission to be creative back. Take a minute to breathe deeply into your diaphragm and get more oxygen to your body, especially the brain. Ask God or the Universe or whomever for some Creative Flow. Say thanks in advance for it, then **take a walk**. (I like to hike a short little mountain outside my neighborhood or bounce on the trampoline for a few to get a lot of energy moving thru me... Because of the hydration and enticing scents of fun body/hair products, I always get a TON of creative ideas in the shower... sometimes I have to write them down in nothing but a towel because so much as come to me and I don't want to miss the fresh excitement of it... **I only write with colored sharpies and use unlined paper, because I don't want any boundaries and I'm not in 3rd grade anymore. I can do what I want!)**

Not every creative idea comes to fruition... It's the possibility and the FLOW of creativity you're looking for here. **That's what you want to be open to!** The flow will bring you more and more ideas, and some you WILL take action on... some of those will need to go back to the drawing board, and some of them will develop into the BIG DADDIES of success. Creative flow brings all this your way. (*Plus how do you think this book got written?? You guessed it... that very process!*)

PURPLE-COW-NESS

Resource: Seth Godin, Purple Cow. Brilliant book. **It's all about being remarkable.** Remarkable as in one-of-a-kind, excellent, and extraordinary in some way, or as I see it, hopefully MANY ways. Nothing new was developed without a lot of flops, mistakes, and courage, so your Purple-Cow-Ness doesn't have to happen right away. But it does need to happen.

You may say that I'm a dreamer.

But I'm not the only one.

- John Lennon

Just as everyone has a unique contribution to make to the world, everyone has a way to be remarkable, or that Purple Cow. Like I said before, our girl Snooki is a Purple Cow, and she's compounded success after success, much to the shock and awe of the entire world, because of it. Hollywood is full of brown-cow beautiful and mostly politically correct, and Snooki rocked that to the core with her differences! Her mannerisms might be a bit questionable, but her remarkableness is undeniable. <<sigh>> In *The Answer* (John Assaraf and Murray Smith) I read about a Pediatric Dentist who took what would be a "brown-cow" kind of business and made it Purple in a way that benefited himself and a ton of other people in the process:

A Win-Win Situation always pays off.

He doubled and then tripled his business by creatively problem-solving, investing in a risk, and doing something absolutely no other Dentist was doing... he hired a limousine service to pick-up/drop-off kids at school for their appointments. **Win**: Parents don't have to take time off work. **Win**: Every single kid wanted to go the Dentist in the Limo. **Win**: His client list doubled, then tripled. He had become a Purple-Cow: something different and unique and something people were talking about. Did he have to take a risk? Yes. And he had to put extra effort and money up-front to make it happen (EVEN WHEN HE DIDN'T KNOW IF IT WOULD PAYOFF!)... he had to buy extra insurance, get waiver forms, research limo companies, poll parents do see if they would go for something like this... turned out it was a yes, it worked out for everyone and became a great thing for everyone involved. High-five!

Q: What happens when people think outside the box?

A: Cool shit.

I invite you to meet some fascinating peeps:

Jessica Kerbawy always loved Art, but never thought there was a "real future" in it... adrift with that mentality (I had it too, girl!), she declared 1 (nope) 2 (nuh-huh) 3 (wrong again) 4 (dear God) 5 very random degrees before **happily** returning to her original passion - Art! (Ahhhh, this story sounds a wee bit familiar to mine, Miss Jessica!) Elementary Ed, Religious Studies, Business, Interior Design, & Horticulture were all points on the path, but <u>finally</u> listening to that **inner voice**, Jessica acquired 2 associate degrees in Art History & Fine Art and started her own Graphic Design Business.

YAY! With lots of new-found creative freedom, she was inspired to experiment with an old-time friend from all of our childhood's, the Crayola Crayon.

Look what this crazy cool chick did:

(you: **OMG, I FREAKING LOVE IT!** me: **OMG, I KNOW! I LOVE IT TOO!**)

On a whim, She **created** Melted Crayon Art, and gets **boatloads** of compliments and attention from guests, selling her Art at Festivals and on her Etsy Site, JKCREATE. In less than two weeks, one of her images had over 4,000 views, and another was cycling through both Pinterest and StumbleUpon. What's Jess got to say about all this?? **"Since "giving in" to my inner Artist, I have been the most creative in my life, each work day feels like playtime, and I couldn't be happier!"** Exactly. And the world is a better place, with cooler shit in it, because of her. That so rocks! You can find more at www.jkcreate.net. (Photo credit by CLE Photography and then I got my hands on it and www.picnik.com –ed all over it... a black n white pic just doesn't do her work justice, so I truly urge you to check out her website. You'll smile. She's amazingface!)

$$* * * * *$$

Brian Spencer for Vurtego Pogo Sticks. www.vurtegopogo.com These are so sick, I can't even stand it. I first heard of Vurtego on ABC's Shark Tank, where my son was in awe of these sticks. Brian's business is in the Extreme Sports niche, and he & his team of peeps re-engineered the pogo stick to a whole new level. **Purple Cow!** (They literally bounce like 10+ feet in the air, and the pros do flips and all kinds of tricks on these bad boys.) They're now selling in several countries, and I'm getting one for me and my son when he's just a little older. *I am secretly just as excited about that as he is! For the record, my son isn't allowed to flip on these till he's older. I'm not ready for all that...*

© www.vurtegopogo.com – it came from their website –

*****

Taylor Reeve. Chick Artist. Southern California. Paints on soles of shoes, among other things. Yes. I know. I love it too!

Straight from her Facebook page: (you can find her on Etsy too!)

Putting her **vibrant**, stylized twist on just about everything in her path has made Taylor Reeve's artwork pervasive in the youth culture movement of Southern California. Drawing on a wide array of influences from **street** and **pop art** to graffiti, **tattoo** and kustom kulture, Taylor has developed a unique style that marks her work as wholly her own.

Taylor currently works with Quicksilver, Dragon Optical, Osiris, and SkullCandy! Her signature pieces of Quicksilver men's outerwear hit stores this winter! Her Dragon sunglasses and moto goggles are available now as well!

*****

IM**POSSIBILTY** AND BOUNDARIES, as a final thought… Don't

buy into either one. It is virtually impossible to bend metal and make it fly, or float for that matter. It's impossible to turn a switch and make it light in a dark room. It's an outlandish, ridiculous, and laughable idea that almost every American home will have a personal computer. There is no way on earth people of the world will be able to answer a phone call away from their landline.

Listen to the MUSTN'Ts, child,

Listen to the DON'Ts

Listen to the SHOULDN'Ts,

The IMPOSSIBLES, the WON'Ts

Listen to the NEVER HAVEs

Then listen close to me –

Anything can happen, child, **ANYTHING** can be.

- Shel Silverstein

CHAPTER **FOUR:** PAY THE PRICE

You pay for everything.

EVERYTHING.

You either pay with your **money**, your **time**,

your **health** (physical/mental)

or your **soul/happiness**.

This is a fact. With any and every decision you make from now on, apply this universal truth, accept your choice, and then move forward without bitching or second-guessing yourself. There are no right or wrong answers here in the choices... it's up to you and different for everyone. The principle of PAY THE PRICE is what you need to accept and apply as you make choices from now on, because that's what you can't get away from, sweetcheeks.

Every "Master" was once a disaster.

- T. Harv Ecker

THE MOST BEAUTIFUL PEOPLE
WE HAVE KNOWN
ARE THOSE WHO HAVE KNOWN DEFEAT,
KNOWN SUFFERING,
KNOWN STRUGGLE,
KNOWN LOSS,
AND HAVE FOUND THEIR WAY
OUT OF THE DEPTHS.
THESE PERSONS HAVE AN APPRECIATION,
A SENSITIVITY,
AND AN UNDERSTANDING OF LIFE
THAT FILLS THEM WITH COMPASSION,
GENTLENESS,
AND A DEEP LOVING CONCERN.
BEAUTIFUL PEOPLE DO NOT JUST HAPPEN.

- ELIZABETH KUBLER ROSS

Everyone pays a price.

Example 1:

My pipe bursts under my sink. I can pay a plumber, which **costs** me money, but **saves** me time and makes me happy, plus keeps me healthy so things don't get all moldy and gross. I can fix it myself (*not really, let's be serious here*), which **saves** me money but **costs** me time **and happiness** because I don't have the slightest interest in this activity. Plus it'll probably take me a thousand years, things will get unhealthy, moldy, and gross, and I could hurt myself. Or eff up my nails, which isn't good news either. I can do nothing, which saves me money, saves me time, but **costs** me a lot of happiness and most def is not good for mine or anyone else's health in the house.

Example 2:

I can buy a large house with a large yard in the Midwest, pay medium prices for gas, and use my heat and air-conditioning a lot, which **costs** a medium amount of money, in respect to the rest of the country. I have to deal with snow/icy winters, which *might* really piss me off. I could have allergies there or other health issues, or I could be healthy as a horse. I *might* be happy there, or the big house in a place I'm not crazy about *might* **cost** me a lot in the soul/happiness area. I can buy (or rent) a smaller house on a smaller piece of property in Southern California, **pay** a lot for gas, but hardly ever need to run any heat or air-conditioning, **saving** money there. I live near the beach and don't ever have to scrape my windshield or freeze my cute little buns off. This *might* **make** me extremely happy $(!!!)$, or I *might* long for sprawling countryside (PS – I don't), which in turn would **cost** me the soul/happiness price. I *might* be super healthy here and learn how to juice thanks to Kris Carr's "Crazy Sexy Diet" (which I sincerely recommend), or the air *might* be smoggier and not good for me…. *(If I were in LA… we're pretty good in San Diego)* This scenario *might* go on and on….

Example 3:

I have a job working for "the man" that **pays** me money every 2 weeks. It **costs** me 8+ hours a day, at least 5 days a week in my time, and I hate it with every fiber of my soul… in this scenario, I'm paying a pretty high price with my time and soul for a very mediocre i.e. "safe" paycheck and lifestyle. This could **cost** me my health, and I could end up in the ER with kidney stones and look like a sick hag at 30 because I'm having anxiety attacks and can't sleep at night before filing for divorce. *(Hypothetically.)*

Or I could work diligently and creatively, learn some enormously helpful skills, read some brilliant books like this one right here, stretch outside my comfort zone, and eventually quit my sucky day job. This will **cost** me some money (in books, education, mentors and maybe a coach/consultants), **cost** me some time (a lot at first, and then less and less over time), but **make** me ridiculously happy, content, fulfilled, inspired and creative… all of which **make** me waaayyyy more healthy and **saves** me money in the long run with healthcare costs while extending my life.

Alright, so you get the picture. When you've got some inner conflict or struggle with a big choice ahead, or even a small one like grilled chicken at home or a big fat burger at In n' Out (I'm not judging either way, as a matter of fact now I REALLY want In n' Out!), apply the logic of PAY THE PRICE, make your bed, then lay in it. **By the by, life is full of choices and you'll always have another one**

right around the corner, so if you chill out & accept the price, you'll have far less angst over the decisions. Remember the answers and choices in life are different for everyone, no right or wrong. Use this:

My Choice Right Now	Costs Me	Saves Me
My Money		
My Time		
My Health		
My Soul/Happiness		

Some Staggering "Fun Facts" (from Google, Huffington Post, U.S. Department of Labor Statistics, AOL... all that.)

- 85% of College Graduates will have over $100,000 in debts and end up moving back in with their parents
- About half of all College Grads who DO get jobs (up to 20% do not) make on average $11/hr. (For perspective, my 22 yr. old Nanny who never went to college but is AMAZING at what she does charges $16/hr and drives a Hummer.)
- Unemployment is the highest it's been in over 2 Decades, and jobs **ARE NOT** coming back
- More than 55% of Employed people HATE their job, and another 18% are "Severely to Moderately Dissatisfied"
- Studies show we are becoming a "Forced Entrepreneurship" Economy, where people need to CREATE their own job opportunities because "Corporate America" will never exist again like it once did
- College Grads have **ON AVERAGE** 3-5 **career** changes in their lifetimes and 10-14 **job** changes by the time they're 38 years old
- Companies are outsourcing (overseas) and CONTRACTING employees for their expertise more now than ever in history because it saves them a ton on $$$ on taxes and Worker's Compensation Insurance, Health Insurance, etc... which means, **MIDDLE-**

MANAGEMENT EASY STREET JOBS FOR COLLEGE GRADS ARE A THING OF THE PAST AND NEVER COMING BACK!

- If you are not positioned to make money and a career on your OWN terms, you need to prepare yourself for a LOT of unforeseen, unplanned, and unwanted changes on other people's terms... (and P.S., that's not where you want to be... that's a victim roll when you should be the Oscar-Nominated Lead Male/Female in the Best Action/Adventure/Drama category.)

To that last bullet point I say, Bring It! I think if people are empowered to intelligently put their passion as their business into the world, the cooler and more creative society we can become. That means more re-engineering and re-thinking a lot of old school stuff and making them AWESOME again. You have these ideas! It's time to bust them out and show the world what you're made of! Afterwards, let's meet for Happy Hour and get some Margaritas or somethin'. Ole, amigos!

THE "USELESS" MASTER'S DEGREE, More Thoughts:

Every year people plan out their future and pursue their so-called "dreams", with many parents and young adults pushing for college degrees and paper accolades as a targeted goal... But they do so without putting the proper thought and effort into the PURPOSE of their education. Education is learned in many ways, and the lecture halls of a slow-to-change University isn't always the right answer.

These days, it's often the WRONG answer!

Every single year, people with prestigious degrees struggle with making ends meet and even worse yet, getting a job where they can use their degree... or want to!

Most young adults either don't have a clue what they really want to do with their lives, or they know but haven't developed all the emotional and developmental skills needed to passionately and successfully pursue their true dream. (The latter one – that was me.)

So they go to college like their parents want, switch majors often (also me!), and end up just wanting to graduate in *something* and get a "job" to start making money and living their "grown-up" life. Not the most fulfilling, but not the most horrific plan... for the 80s and 90s. Today, it ain't gonna fly:

- Tuition has gone up more than 1000% in the past couple decades, while College Graduate's pay salary has only gone up about 300% (same as standard inflation)
- It used to take an average College Grad 7-10 years to pay off Student Loans, and now it takes 25-30
  - It can take longer to pay for a 4 year degree than a house
    - As a Nation, we have more Student Loan Debt than Home Mortgage Debt
- College Grads used to find high-paying Middle-Management type jobs, which have almost all been eliminated in the Great Recession and this new economy
  - Universities cannot keep up with the fast-paced technical changes in the world, namely the niches/trends, the demand for applied knowledge, and the life/work balance our society is gravitating towards
- Most careers today can be better learned by real-world training and experience, and many of the fastest growing industry leaders have not gone to college (or dropped out)... ala Steve Jobs, Bill Gates, Mark Zuckerburg...

Now I'm not against a college education entirely, but PLEASE KNOW that the marketplace does not pay for a degree, they pay for experience. Every job worth pursuing comes with a learning curve and an establishing period. Even people who get a Master's Degree in Business and/or Marketing (like me!) know absolutely nothing when it comes to the real-world and internet... until they get into the thick of things day in and day out and actually DO THE WORK. As a matter of fact, most people who have an MBA end up coming face to face with the sad reality that their degree means absolutely nothing when it comes to PPC, Blogging and Massive Lead Generation in the online marketing world.

And in 2011 and beyond, you need to be online to make money... in ANY field.

(Unless you want to be a Himalayan Monk. You might be able to stay offline for that.)

Freedom is the goal, not business and not a paper degree. The "You Need A College Degree" Myth is being pushed and perpetuated by Colleges and Universities... who are a BUSINESS and are in the BUSINESS of making money.

Historically, since the Great Depression – not like since the beginning of time, which many incorrectly think and assume, College Grads made more money than non.

Not necessarily today, though, and definitely not necessarily in the future!

ALL PEOPLE, INCLUDING YOU, will be better served, more successful, and have a much better lifestyle (income, health, wealth, and personal fulfillment level) if you take the time to intelligently pursue your real dreams and purpose before jumping into a ton of debt and a construction-delayed route of "your path."

If your **passion** whole-heartedly depends on Higher Education, then by all means, my friend, dive in! Whaaaaa?? I mean, if your truest desire is to be a Doctor and heal people... then you need to go to College and Pre-Med and get your shit done. If your truest passion is Law and you daydream of courtroom litigation... then you need to go to College. Do your thang! If you want nothing more than to design spectacular bridges and aircraft, for the love of all that's holy, **please** go to College! But if you don't really know what you want to do, you're doing it for someone else or because of the "you need a college degree" myth, or just to "get a good job" at some big company, then you need to think again.

Think about the debt you're going to accrue and the burden you're going to create for yourself/your parents. If you are a parent, think about why you're sending your kid to college. Is it the historical data from the Great Depression to the Great Recession about College Grads earning more wages?? If so, just realize we've become a new society.

Things have changed, whether you want to hear it or not.

I have a 4 year degree in Education, and I use it to educate in the real-world rather than in the traditional classroom. I educate from my personal research and real-world business experience, not from the classes I took on phonics at Arizona State. (Go Devils!) I have a Master's in Business Development and Marketing, which I used about 3 ounces of in my actual career path... the rest of my kick-assness came from learning from real-world coaches and business people, and it opened up my entire life and career with abundance... it taught me to do what I love, do it with integrity and pride and passion, and the money will follow.

Know what you're doing. **But more importantly, why.**

I'm all for the college experience, but nowadays it carries a hefty price-tag and doesn't guarantee for one second any employment, fulfillment, job security, or financial stability.

ONLY YOU CAN DETERMINE THAT, AND IT TAKES SOME EFFORT.

I had the BEST time at ASU, and have some life-long friends and laugh out loud experiences and memories from those 4 years of life. I'm not against any of that, but I do think there are some foundational steps and new wisdom to plant in the minds of people before they just blindly "go to school." Looking back I wish I had done a lot of things differently. I wish I had traveled the world more and done a little more for the community rather than partying my ass off and paying $150 a pop on fake id's. I wish I had learned about Life Coaches, Business Coaches, and Mentors back then while working on my tan lines. (I always had the most fantastic tan!) I wish I had puked a little more from dysentery with the Peace Corps than from keggers. But because I can look back and know these things now, I have the opportunity to pass my wisdom and knowledge onto many many others with the intent of opening eyes to a fantastic lifestyle based on real-life.

And it's effing awesome on this side of things, by the by! Come join me!

A LESSON IN **PAY-THE-PRICE-PERSPECTIVE**

One of the smartest and most focused business men I know is **Eric Reese**, who happens to be the Music Producer and Owner/Entrepreneur/Mogul-Building CEO behind **Pearl Harbor Entertainment**. We initially met and collaborated on the original Painted Laugh™ almost 3 years ago with my own son's recording. If you don't know what **The Painted Laugh**™ is yet, let me explain (plus you can check us out at our website listed below.)

Here's **The Painted Laugh** story:

When my son had just turned 3 years old, we were in my studio painting, which we did often. I would often strip him down to just his undies, then pop in the bathtub for clean-up. Too many unsupervised moments went by... and he was way too quiet... I found him naked, about to finish painting his entire body "like Superman!" he exclaimed happily. What. The. Hell?? I laughed. He laughed. And in the split second I decided to let him finish instead of making him stop. He was just so stinkin' proud of himself, and freaking adorable to boot. We had the best moment, parent & child, and it's one of my most profound memories... then that little sh*t turned on me (and by "little sh*t" I really mean "angel-face-love-of-my-life-and-giver-of-some-stretchmarks-who-is-totally-worth-it-smooch-smooch"), covered in paint, and tried to hug me/grab me/get me... I bolted! He laughed SOOOO hard, chasing me around that studio while I pretended to scream and get away. In that moment, I saw his laughter in the air for the first time. The colors of his laugh were blue, purple, and yellow swirls, and they filled the entire room, like smoke might, but without being foggy or cloudy... I mean crystal clear. I grabbed my phone, recorded his laughter as he continued to chase me, and snapped a couple flicks (they're on the website, www.ThePaintedLaugh.com). I knew I had to put his laugh to canvas. I had to paint it. I knew that day, God had given a direct gift to me to bring into this world: Painted Laughter. It didn't exist before that day, before me, before my son... I had no choice but to bring it into the world! God hadn't given it to me to sit on, for His/Her sake!!! (I felt a little like her majesty, Oprah, if you must know.)

The thing is, I was super scared to do it... first of all, I felt like a compete whackadoo, talking about "seeing" sounds for the first time. I had "seen" loud, abrupt, unpleasant noises all my life... but never realized nobody else did. I've always been really sensitive to volume/noise, and it's gotten worse in adulthood. I can't take it very long – I will totally burn out and over-stimulate... Why?? Because as I pursued The Painted Laugh and spoke of this phenomenon to more and more people, the Universe delivered me the gift of knowledge. I have Synesthesia. I was so pleased, so relieved, and so eager to learn more. I felt instantly understood and not one bit more crazy than usual.

::Synesthesia::

A neurological condition in which the stimulation of 1 sense triggers/crosses in the brain, creating automatic and involuntary experiences in a second sense or cognitive pathway. There are several different types of Synesthesia, resulting in numerous different symptoms/abilities. Translation: my senses cross-over sometimes, and because my type is Sound-Color, I can "see" sound in the air as different colors and patterns. (Gooooo, me!)

Fan-fucking-tastic! I'm now super excited to bring this in the world and talk about it! Buuuuuuuuut, I had no idea how to do it. That's incorrect. First, I thought it would be easy and I would overtake the world. I thought, who in their right mind wouldn't fall madly in love with this and want their own child's laugh painted?? This is the new sliced bread! And I'm the one who is supposed to do something about it! Then THAT'S when it dawned on me that I had no idea how to do it... That's when my real-world education began, and I decided I was blazing my own trail. I was the Anti-Gray-Suit-Campaign of 1. Like in the Army, only prettier, and with jewelry and stilettos... and this whole book is about what happened from there!

www.thepaintedlaugh.com

So anywho, back to **Eric...** who is brilliant, driven, talented, focused, and yet for all he's accomplished, he is humble and introspective as well. I asked him to contribute some advice for this book, and he gave me this wisdom to share with the world on **PAY-THE-PRICE PERSPECTIVE**...

© Pearl Harbor Entertainment

"

A person needs to keep **perspective** when they're going after their dreams. You're

building something forever, if you're doing it right! **It's the little things day after day that build the empire.**

You're doing things *today* that will be hugely important in 2-3-5-10-15 years, and other people are going to make you doubt that. The thing is, if you were becoming a Doctor, they wouldn't expect you to do surgery

tomorrow. A "Doctor" is a socially-accepted dream, and it's normal and expected to go to school for 8-10 years, make $0, and accumulate a LOT of debt. Then a Doctor has residency, and long hours/shifts... and no

one would ever try to deter them from THAT! Keep that **perspective!** If you have a dream and **passion**, and put the same time, money and dedication someone becoming a Doctor puts into their

dream, would you have a huge chance at success?? **Yes.** But people try to deter you from the dream. They expect you to be famous in a day, and those doubts, that negativity seeps in... Don't let it! **Don't do it to yourself, either.** There is NO over-night success... the people you think have "over-night success" have been working for months and years to get to that point. **Keep the Doctor-like perspective.** You don't apply to Med School and perform surgery the next day, week, month, or year. Put your time in, and keep your perspective. You put time in. You develop and hone your

skills. You pick a specialty. You work hard... and then, **Success will come.**

All great **achievements** require time.

- Maya Angelou

***

ALIGNEMENT: A Big Deal

Strap in. This is important. You'll notice my type is big, highlighting that fact.

If you don't <u>love</u> what

you do... if you don't <u>love</u> your life... and I mean **LOVE!** If

you're not crazy excited passionate invigorated engaged and peacefully happy & fulfilled in what you do,

you will **never** be in a state of **flow**. Flow is present contentment & gratitude right now, with

grand, vivid visions for the future. Flow engages & fuels a legacy and allows you to make a unique impact

with your life. Flow moves forward. Flow is part of Alignment. You have the choice to be part of your

flow. You have the choice right now! It's **present in every single one of us**, and it's part of the

connection we **ALL** have in the human race: the desire for balance, abundance, fulfillment, and happiness. (Those things appear/are defined differently for each of us, but the **DESIRE** is the same.)

You will never feel **complete** if one of those is missing in your life. The only way to make that

happen is to spend time **aligning with your true purpose** in this life.

It's not easy, because in our Society we've actually been trained and conditioned to ignore it! We're taught to feel guilty about wanting it all: Balance. Happiness. Money. Family. Love. Health. Spirituality...

we've been taught that it doesn't really exist or is selfish & irresponsible to pursue, **OR**, it's destined for some other people but not for you. But I'm telling you that it is! It is meant for you, you reading this, and it is possible if you take the time to straighten all your junk out. You were meant to read this book, these words, and get the feeling that I really am talking to you. Absorb some possibility right now. Open

your mind to who you are really meant, no, **required** to become in this lifetime. Who you wanted

to be as a kid, and how you imagined life would feel when you daydreamed all those years ago. Invest a little time in yourself, and in those dreams. We've been incorrectly programmed to ignore those things, but right now, let's **NOT**.

When I first began this awakening for myself, I was in a really sad, dark place. I was miserable, drained, unfulfilled, and then unhealthy... totally stressed out. I hated my job, and was about to end a marriage that just wasn't working out, no matter how hard we tried. And we did! We had a gorgeous young son, and he was our gift from our time together... but the marriage itself was suffering and beyond repair. It wasn't about marriage; it was about us being 2 totally disconnected people with polar opposite beliefs

and visions and risk assessment. I was *forcing* everything at that time... NO FLOW AT ALL!!! I

was forcing a career I hated, my time and energy, my happiness, my marriage... and right now, sitting

where I am today, I can tell you that **there is no way to compare the difference**

in a forced life vs. a flowing life. The more I trusted myself, my intuition, and started

courageously building the life & dreams I truly **wanted** (for me and my son), the more power and

assurance I felt deep in my core. I was aligning, saying yes to new ideas, and for the first time I **knew**

in my bones I was on the right path. I was connecting to myself, and at the same time something bigger than myself. A lot of fears and inadequacies and lack of know-how came to the surface, so I know where you're at & what you're feeling right now.

Your Comfort Zone   Where the Magic Happens

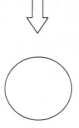
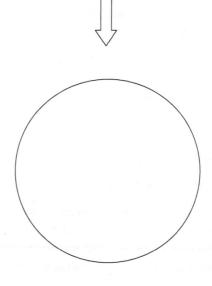

What matters to me, and probably what matters a lot to you too if you're here, is living life awake! And if you're not fully activated with your ideal lifestyle/career/passion balance, and don't find yourself out-of-your-skull-happy, than you haven't allowed yourself to align properly yet, and you absolutely deserve it! **It is the nicest gift you can give yourself, your family/spouse/kids, your career, and our planet. We're all in this together, and aligned people do extraordinary things!** It is MY true purpose and mission in life to help people around the globe to awake, align, and contribute their unique gift/purpose to our world. Our kids deserve it, and future generations will benefit from this awakening happening right now. When I first came to realize this, I was all, whaaaaa?!?! Me?!?! All these voices and insecurities came to the surface... "Who do you think you are?"... "C'mon Sonja, you're just some everyday normal chick, and people will judge you, think your crazy, reject you and these ideas..." We've all had those voices, and so many times we have the opportunity to either let them stop us, OR MOVE FORWARD. These are defining moments, when we say yes, and move into something bigger than we ever thought possible. These are the moments where I wish I could insert dramatic & climactic background into my everyday life.

So <u>how do we say yes</u>??

Like this: 1. Deep breath   2. Yes

Just like that. Then take the time to write down everything you LOVE. Love love crazy love. It doesn't matter what it is. Write down everything you HATE. Fucking Hate! Hate so much you absolutely will not accept it anymore in your life and in your future. And keep reading, because we're going to highlight and touch on some other things you need to take the time to do... as you do them, you need to be honest. When you are aligning, it takes time and courage because it's all on your own... YOUR dreams, desires, and intuition... not your parents', your church's, your neighbor's, your friend's, your spouse's... and that's really difficult. I won't sugar coat that pill at all. It's very hard to make choices that are best for you when a lot of people near you are going to disapprove, disagree, or try to talk you out of them. But know this: Their opinions are about them, not you. They are expressing how THEY would handle being in YOUR situation... That's what advice is!!! But they aren't you, and they don't have to be there at the end of the road (whenever that is), when you have regrets and dreams and ambitions and a life you never had the courage to live. That's no good. Don't do that to yourself. This is your real life, right now. **You're already paying the price in one way or another.** You might as well pay the prices for what you really want instead of what you really don't! Makes sense, no?!?!

Do you know how much energy you spend arguing with your own intuition, pushing it away, ignoring it, suffocating it, strangling the life out of it?? Well I don't either, actually. I was hoping one of us would. Totally kidding. It's different for everyone. I used to spend ungodly amounts of my precious life and energy arguing with mine. Now I don't spend any. I'm not an arguer, by nature, and learned to make friends with my inner voices and intuition. I decided we'll be spending the long haul together, and we should be drinking buddies instead of frenemies all the time.

What are you feeling right now about what I said?? Are you saying yes, or resisting, feeling uneasy, fearful, judgmental, or uncomfortable?? What would it feel like instead to make decisions in life, not second guess yourself anymore, and not waffle back and forth?? You will **know**, when you follow and befriend your intuition and not push away what you REALLY want to do in your life, every decision you make is the right one. How awesome is that?!?! Well, it's true, too. It takes time, but you actually can choose to live your life that way... like I do. <<wink>>

TIME FOR SOME Q & As BETWEEN US FRIENDS

You: But Sonja, I don't ever want to be my own boss, I don't want to start a business, and I'm NOT an Entrepreneur in any way.

Translation: I don't know how to be or wouldn't want to be the boss of me.

Me: Ok, let me start by quoting Tony Hsieh, young, self-made Billionaire and CEO of Zappos.com. Think shoes. (Fun Fact: He claims to only own 3 pairs of shoes, not including flip-flops.) Tony says your goal, everyone's goal, should always be to be your own boss. Always. Here's why: If you are dependent on a job for your paycheck to live, you are disempowered. If you then buy a house and need that paycheck to pay your bills, you've also become enslaved and will feel trapped and severely limited in your choices. If there is anyone in our country who still believes in 100% job security over the recession fiasco the last few years, well then you are delusional on top of everything else. (Want to make the scenario even more sporty?!?! Hellz yeah you do, you're starting to take after me already!!! Let's say you and your spouse buy a nice, big house that requires BOTH paychecks coming in to maintain... Well, we all can see how that'll play out in the event of the marriage becoming unhealthy. Double stuck!)

This position of dependency, disempowerment, and entrapment actually changes the way your brain operates. Guess what?? It doesn't alter it in a good way. This kind of conditioned state actually diminishes both cognitive abilities **and** our primal instincts/drive to achieve, aspire, create, and align with a purpose bigger than ourselves. We actually become conditioned to want, care, and exceed our highest potentials. We kinda become permanent autopilot. That's sad. That's, like creative impotence. Everything about this situation leads to a person feeling exhausted, frustrated, overwhelmed, unfulfilled, and severly UNDER-employed, meaning not allowed or able to use their full arsenal of mind-blowing skills and personality characteristics.

Dependency + Disempowerment + Entrapment won't ever = Alignment + Creative Flow

Now let's say you love your job, career, boss or company, and you feel really fulfilled and already pretty much aligned. That is awesome, it
DOES happen, and serious high-five to you guys out there! BUT, I still believe you should be exploring these ideas and setting yourself up with passion online as well, even if you don't do it to make any money yet. The reason is twofold: First, your paycheck is going to have a cap, even at the tippity-top, if you even make it that far... just knowing that fact will alter your mindset & set you up with limiting beliefs of what you're worth. (Disempowerment.) Second, there is no job security anymore, and your dream job could actually disappear tomorrow... and that unemployment picture at the mo' ain't a pretty one! You should always be looking out for yourself, and if you choose to listen to Tony Hsieh's advice (I DO!!!), always have a goal to be your own boss, be in charge of yourself, and be open to make any amount of money you choose.

You: Sonja, all this talk of Millionaires, Billionaires, $$$... you're obsessed with money and materialistic things and you're shallow! There's way more to life than money!

Translation: I don't believe I could ever be a Millionaire/Billionaire myself so I'm going to reject it and justify my own position by taking "the high road" on the issue.

Me: Money isn't everything! Money cannot buy anyone love, health, happiness, fulfillment, soulfulness, or a great sense of humor. That, my love, is ALIGNMENT!!!

This is **exactly** a discussion I had recently with my son regarding money. It's important to me that he has a strong, beneficial relationship with money starting young. He's 6, and can understand what I'm saying, so I don't think you'll have any issues...

> Money cannot buy you happiness or love. Those 2 things come from inside you, from your heart, and those things are up to YOU to find for YOURSELF. No one else can do that for you. Understand that happiness & love are INSIDE of you, not outside in any other erson or any thing you can buy. (I put my hand on his heart when I said this, looked him in his big blue eyes (he got those from me!), and I smiled! This lesson is important while being extremely beautiful! You should smile too, as a matter of fact. Right now! Smile about money right now!) What money <u>does</u> give you are choices, opportunity, and more power to make a significant difference in the world. Money opens up the entire world to you with the choices, opportunities, and experiences you get to have. Money gives us the opportunity to travel to Rio to watch the Summer 2016 Olympics. (Which we're planning to do, because I want him to see the entire world on an elevated level of greatness... I want him to FEEL that energy.) Money gives you the power to decide what's best for you, and gives you options to choose from. Money also gives you the power to positively change other people's lives. Money is a good thing, and I want you to feel the power and excitement of money. (I put 10 $1000 stacks of cash in his little lap... I wanted him to remember this, and believe me, he DOES! His eyes were big. We were both smiling. He smelled the money. He stacked the piles in a couple different ways, built a house. Then we reinforced what we talked about. And he gets it!)

So if your concern is that I talk too much about money or put too much emphasis on it, I would suggest that maybe you're not putting ENOUGH on it for yourself, and that's limiting your beliefs, flow, and ability to have it. #myopiniontakeitorleaveit

You: Sonja, you sound like your telling people to not go to college, step away from their jobs, and then they'll step into abundance & happiness & wealth & health, and that's just not true for most people.

Translation: I don't believe you.

Me: That's 4 things, yo!

1. College is far too expensive, and is a Capitalist Business. Colleges are there to make money, please don't ever let that slide by you for a second, and they do it by perpetuating a myth between parents and children that you need a college degree to succeed, and that isn't true in 2011 and beyond. The rules have changed, thanks to technology and the interweb. Colleges also teach you inside a campus, can't keep any curriculum up with how fast things change today, and teaches a lot of outdated material. College for most 18-22 year olds is a social experiment in new-found freedom and shenanigans, which can be experienced in other, more productive, and more profound ways than by disguising it in "education" and paying thousands of dollars per credit hour. College degrees are a dime a dozen now, and in no way guarantees anyone a good job, or more importantly a job you'll be fulfilled, empowered, and aligned with. Most college graduates accrue about $75,000 of debt, at which time they enter the workforce (dependency) to find a mediocre job that'll probably barely cover basic expenses (limitations). Most of these college grads have no networking experience in the real world, no hands-on education, and no worldly/global insight to contribute (as they've been living their own, sheltered, dorm/campus life)... Right now almost every profession out there has experienced, college grads they're laying off... not a good look for our new college grads, deep in debt, is it?? (Should *some* people go to college?? Yes, absosmurfly. Surgeons, Engineers, Architects, Vets... when your true purpose and alignment require advanced education, then go to college. Most people, however, don't fit into this category. Yes you... you with the partial "Communications" or "Criminal Justice" Degrees before you flunked out your 2nd year.) If you pay tuition, you can get a degree. It isn't special anymore. It doesn't determine your worth and the value you'll give to the world... YOU do!

2. You should always be able to step away from (or get kicked out of) your job and be in a position to move forward for YOURSELF, without having to depend on someone else to employ you. It takes time, and I'm suggesting you start now rather than at a point of crisis down the road. I'm telling you to think about and put time, effort, focus, and investment on your own desires and a lifestyle/ career you would love. No matter if you like, love, or hate your job/career (or lack there of), if you are working for someone else you are at a disadvantage. You may never leave your job, get fired, or set yourself up to make money with what you love... but at least be open to the possibilities and begin to empower yourself somehow. *That* will serve you endlessly in life!

3. Self-made people don't just "step into" wealth, abundance, perfect health, awareness, enlightenment, financial freedom, fabulous shoes and Peach Sangria afternoons... and I'm not suggesting it's an easy, quick trip. I'm saying it takes time, knowledge, strategy, skills (either developing yours or learning from other people who've already done it), effort, action, and a positive mindset. It helps to have a wicked sense of humor too, because you won't believe how much shit goes awry and you find yourself scratching your head. Self-made people make a lot of mistakes, but they learn and develop and keep moving forward anyways. I'm also saying that if you lay the groundwork correctly, align with your very own truth and go for it, you'll be shocked at the abundance that can flow seemingly effortlessly to you. It's like a puzzle where you're trying to force pieces together just to get it done, and then you decide to do it "right," and it goes way smoother... finally you get it all together, and you can't even imagine where you'd be if you kept

trying to squeeze all those wrong pieces together. I'm saying you **won't** automatically "step into" abundance... if you do it right and put the effort & action required into your dreams and career, you WILL **flow** into it over time.

4. It is possible for everyone. If you can't wrap your head around that yet, then you've found your starting point! Don't tell anyone else it's not possible for them because that'll make you a liar.

That's right. I said it! I said it because it **IS** possible for every single person to align their ideal

lifestyle/career/passion and live wide awake, fulfilled, healthy, and happy. It **IS** possible to monetize anything online and make money to support your aligned life. It will take your time and effort, but it **is very possible for every single person.**

You: Sonja... I know a ton of people who had good jobs with great benefits, retired comfortably, sent their kids to college so they could get good jobs, never applied any of your crazy suggestions, and they're doing great! That's how I want it.

Translation: I don't want what you're saying to be true.

Me: Welcome to 2011, almost 2012! Things have changed. I'm not sure if you've noticed or not, but we're coming out of a pretty devastating recession. Catastrophes like that tend to create change, and it's not a bad thing. It serves as a wake up call and provides a shift in awareness. There are learning curves, but embrace the idea of change. Resistance and flow don't mesh. Learn to flow.

You: Sh*t. OK. How do I do this then??

Translation: I hear you cluckin', big chicken.

Translation for that: I'm a little scared, but I know you're right and I hear what you're sayin' about 2011 and change and the future and the New Economy.

Me: Cool. I know you're a little unsure right now, but just move thru those feelings. You've got bigger and better ahead of you! Read on, you extremely intelligent and good-looking individual, you...

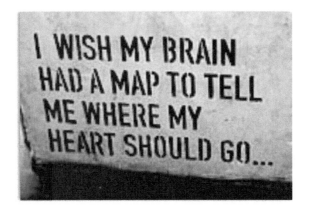

I WISH MY BRAIN HAD A MAP TO TELL ME WHERE MY HEART SHOULD GO....

www.pinterest.com

Barbara Corcoran , NYC Real Estate Mogul and widely known from ABC's Shark Tank as one of, and the only female!, Millionaire-Bazillionaire Investors. If I had to cast a vote, it would be <<yes>> Those People Know What They're Doing. (Opposed to <<nah>> They Got Lucky.) Barbara wrote a book with an amazing title that applies to **KNOWING THYSELF**:

If you don't have big breasts, put ribbons on your pigtails.

(Also known as: Use What You've Got.)

-Barbara Corcoran

"To love oneself is the beginning of a lifelong romance."
— Oscar Wilde

www.piccsy.com

Here's the question I hear all the time: "Sonja, what if I don't *know* what I want?" Variations include: "What if I don't know what I want to do, What if I don't know what I'm good at, or What if I'm not really good at anything special in particular???" (Gasp. These all break my heart a little bit. I never had this problem. I always KNEW what I wanted to do and accomplish, which is why I was probably so tortured with (*and bad at!*) all those other jobs that were so wrong for me. I now can confidently tell people this: **knowing what you want to do** is the greatest **gift** (because some people never take the time to clarify that in their whole life!) and the greatest **curse** (because it's hard to do any other shitty "day job" effectively in your life). A paradox, indeed.

: : PARADOX : :

- a statement that is seemingly contradictory or opposed to common sense and yet is perhaps true

- an argument that apparently derives self-contradictory conclusions by valid deduction from acceptable premises

- one (as a person, situation, or action) having seemingly contradictory qualities or phases

Now back to those questions at hand... I have a plethora of different ways and activities to get to know the real you a little better, which will provide you ideas and options... if you move forward in action, little-by-little, you start to see the path. Your path. **THAT. IS. EXCITING. (!!!)**

I'm giddy for you, just thinking about it!

The first place to start is to list the things you're naturally good at, things you're really **interested in**, things that you could do or talk about for hours with friends, things that you could do or talk about for hours without friends, **things you'd like to become better at**, and things you'd like to learn more about.

The **2** most important days of your life

are the day you are **born**

and the day you find out **why**.

- Mark Twain

If you won the lottery, and could do anything on Earth, **what would you do?** (*Everyone initially thinks "NOTHING!" And "live on a beach!" or the woods, or a mountain cabin, or something of the sort… but that's just the answer because you're overworked, over-stressed, and under-stimulated at the moment…*) Think of a REAL answer to the question. These are probably very close to your

passions. Here are my passions, as an example (highlighted ones were used to create this book):

Being a Parent – Parenthood – Kids – **My** kid

Laughing – Laughter – Comedy – Comedians – Funny Movies – Funny Books

Painting – Art – Interior Design – Architecture – Feng Shui – Having Fresh Flowers around me – Not actually growing said flowers (you'll see evidence of my Lack o' Green Thumb later…) – Typography

Family – Friends – Entertaining – Throwing Parties – Kid's Birthday Party Planning – Cooking – Killer Cocktail Recipes – Happy Hours – Mexican Food

Health & Fitness – Holistic Health – Acupuncture – Massage – Surfing – Stand-Up Paddleboard – Yoga – Kayaking – Wakeboarding – Snowboarding – Mountain Biking – Glamping (Glamour Camping, because I enjoy my creature comforts and I'm not afraid to let the world know this) – Scuba Diving – Snorkeling – Being Tan

Travel – Australia – Fiji – Italy – Spain – Greece – Brazil – Costa Rica – Mexico – Tahiti

Helping Others – Giving Back – Karma – Humane Society – ASPCA – Unicef – World Wildlife Fund – Sea.Thos Foundation – Children's Hospitals – St. Jude's Children's Research Hospitals – Clothes Off Our Back Foundation

Nature – Hiking – Photography – Reading – Personal Growth & Development – Inner Peace – Happiness

Spirituality – Meditation – Affirmations – Visualization - Gratitude

Next, what are some things that other people think **you're good** at, or that you get **compliments** on. Mine, for example:

My *creativity* with The Painted Laugh concept – My actual Artwork

My parenting – My son's manners – My son's school smarts – My son's sense of goodness/right/wrong/justice

My son's birthday parties (both décor and food)

My sense of humor – When I text or bbm (BlackBerry Messenger), **peeps tell me I should write for a living!**

The courage to pursue my dreams and goals and truly become the person I was meant to be

My sense of goodness/right/wrong/decency/justice/generosity

My sense of adventure, open-mindedness, and ability to try new things

My athletic ability (that's not a joke, despite the fact that I like Glamping)

The fact that I **can, will, and want to** do a flip on the trampoline at age 35 (sober, actually)

Which of the many many many unique experiences that you've had, match up and illustrate things on those lists? That's part of **your story**, and this is a <u>big deal</u>... No one on this planet can tell your story, because no one on this planet has had those same experiences. That alone, is inspiring to think about, isn't it?!?! That alone is reason enough for you to **pursue greatness** beyond what you have so far. Your life is the book, and you're writing it. If you don't love the story so far, start a new freaking chapter! Start with one or two things from those lists, and start to develop new parts to your story. Maybe you need new characters and to meet new people. Maybe you want to take a class in something you've always loved but have been afraid, too tired, too busy, embarrassed, nervous, shy, yadda yadda yadda blah blah blah. I don't mean to be hurtful, I'm just pointing out that's the story you're writing, and that's what you're going to go to your grave with. With *that* in mind, **make sure it's what you really want!** No one is going to make the time for you; no one is going to give you what you don't give yourself; no one else is going to grant you permission **but you.** Put your big-girl/big-boy smile on and

do something cool that **you** love. You might find out you love it more, you might find out you love it less, and you might find out you're not a "natural" at it and need some more practice. (*A "natural," by the way, is pretty much bullshit, with very few exceptions. All "naturals" spend more time, focus, and energy on whatever it is they do than you think. Pablo Picasso, for instance, was trained and educated practically since birth by his father, who was a professional artist. As even a very young boy, his father required him to paint, completely paint over, and repaint canvas again and again and again. And we already talked about the story of how hard and long Michael Jordan worked to become such a "natural."*)

Whatever you focus your time and energy on, you will become good at. I know an awful lot of people who focus their time on making excuses for not having enough time/money for things, or worrying about others, or complaining, or being afraid of failure, or hating their job (and eventually hating their daily life – SOOOO SAD!). Guess what they're becoming <u>proficient</u> at? Guess what their expertise is becoming? Exactly.

If this has been you up to now, it's just a matter of re-focus, and it's just one moment at a time. Think about what you're concentrating on at different points of the day, and if it's kind of Hooper-Humperdink-like and not benefiting those things on your list of **passions** in any way, then recognize it, and nicely ask your brain to shift gears and focus.

Try this: "Hi, brain. You're thinking in a different direction than I want to go. I know you're trying to protect me, but it's ok and **I really do want to focus on this new idea right now**, and I'd like you to work with me and be super creative for a little while. Thanks. Love you! Life wouldn't be the same without you! XOXO"

If you've been practicing bad habits, it's going to take some time to train yourself for better ones. One moment at a time at first… soon you really will be conditioning your brain to see more opportunity, trust more people (ESPECIALLY YOURSELF!), and let more creative ideas flow thru you.

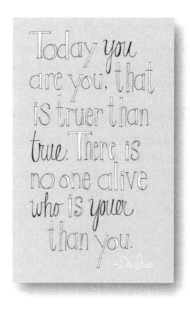

Today you are you, that is truer than true. There is no one alive who is youer than you.
– Dr. Seuss

I always like to find out more about **ME**, read about personalities, take quizzes, etc.... On Facebook, which Muppet were you?? (*I was Fozzie Bear*) What 80s song were you?? (I was Journey's *Don't Stop Believin'*... fitting, I know!) So if you like that too, here are a couple websites I've found that I really like.

I truly feel like I've learned interesting nuances and tendencies about myself and it explains A LOT! It interests me, but it also can catapult me over hurdles and tough situations. (*Me: Hey. Me: Hey. Me: Soooo, you still haven't finished the book yet, and you're emailin' it up with somebody about ANOTHER new project idea. Me: I know. Me: That's kind of your Modus Operandi (Mode of Operation, or "M.O." when I'm rapping), friend. You have a tendency to go balls out on a project, then start a new one before finishing the first. Me: I know. I really want to finish the book too because it rocks. Me: It really does. So let's turn off Fashion Police, and put new-cool-idea on simmer for the mo'. Me: Cool, you're right. Thanks. P.S. Did you see what she was wearing?? Feece! Me: Totalllly. Who lets her go out in that ish?? Now turn it off. Me: <<click>>*)

COLORSTROLOGY

It's Astrology mixed with Color Theory, and it's rad. Quick & Dirty: there's a color frequency that corresponds to the position of the sun on the day you were born, or somethin' like that. Each day of the year has a color that you will naturally be drawn to and vibe with, which affects your personality as much as your Astrological sign can. Mine?? Freakin' dead on, one of my fave colors, and one I paint with alllllll theeeeeee tiiiiiiiime. (*My birthday & Colorsrology?? June 11th, Sunset Gold, and don't be silly, YES of course you can send me gifts!*)

www.colorstrolgy.com and the book available at Amazon.com and other retailers by the same name. (Author Michele Bernhardt.)

PERSONALITY TESTS

There's a really good one I found thru Danielle LaPorte's Spark Kit. **You should check Danielle's blog out for sure**.

WWW.WHITEHOTTRUTH.COM

She's wicked smart, one of my most favorite writers, and basically the chick I wanna be when I grow up. Her writing style, you'll see, is so much like mine, except way better. She writes all the time and for a living mostly, but I don't think she paints, and I do, so I'm pretty ok with her being a lot better than me. I enjoy learning from her, and the personality test she pointed to was revealing. I'd take it if I were you, and keep in mind when you answer the questions to **be honest**. It's not Harvard. You're not going to fail anything. It'll ask you questions like how you would *first react to blahbedy blah blah*, and I would have to keep myself in check and be like, *Sonja, you would FIRST be envious, AND THEN YOU'D BE STOKED FOR SOMEONE ELSE if blahbedy blah blah and you know it, so answer the question honestly (not how you "want" to react)... (True. <<Sigh>>)*

The Enneagram (FREE Test)

http://www.eclecticenergies.com/enneagram/test.php (I like Test 2: compare different actions/reactions)

Aura Tests (it's FREE, too)

http://www.AuraColors.com

(I'm Yellow/Violet, with a very strong Blue and some Abstract Tan undertones.)

Bottom Line:

No one can say what you say, do what you do, teach what you teach, and be who you be (whaaa?? haha) better than you. You really are the only "you" this world is going to ever get, and once you give yourself permission to roll with it, you've got some uniqueness that our world needs. Someone, somewhere, is waiting for exactly what you have to share. (*Like Brian's killer pogo-stick, or my Painted Laughs, or Eric's and Esjay's and Sylvia J's music, or Tammi's & Sarah's messages and leadership, or Taylor's shoes, or my brother's passion for travel, or any & everything else people share with the world. They're sharing their* brilliance, *and you need to find yours and share it too.*)

You need to. YOU need to. You NEED to. **YOU NEED TO!**

CHAPTER **SIX:** VISION AND OTHER SPIDEY SENSES

The world promises you comfort,

but you were not made for comfort.

YOU were made for **GREATNESS**.

- Pope Benedict XVI

This quote just tickles me every time I read it. The Pope! He would physically cringe at the appalling strings of profanity I've been known to line up, the amount of cleavage **OR** leg I show off when out with my guy or the girls for cocktails (*PLEASE NOTE THE* **"OR"** *SITUATION HERE LADIES: IT'S AN* **OR***, NOT AN AND! One or the other… one or the other!*), and the tattoos I happily sport on my body. Yet I had to include The Pope's quote here because it rings true, it shows that it's really not only your "path" but actually part of God's* bigger plan for us all. And lastly I included it because the Pope, who would venomously disapprove of so many things I say and do on a daily basis, is on the same page with me here. High-five, Pope Benedict the whatevers your number is. (*I actually CAN read Roman Numerals, but it's not as funny.*)

*Remember to please insert God/Goddess/Buddha/Allah/Mother Nature/The Universe/or nothing in this space.

IF YOU ARE *"COMFORTABLE"* WITH **YOUR VISION** OF THE **FUTURE**

THEN IT IS NOT **BIG ENOUGH!**

A **GO-BIG** SCENARIO:

I emailed Ivanka Trump, Donald Trump's daughter, directly. I also called Kris Jenner (Kardashian) on her cell phone (left a message) and snail-mailed her a Press Kit about me and my work to her HOME address, which is completely unlisted. BOOM! Talk about ballsy, right?!?! I'm gonna have to run this book cover idea and a chapter or two by Chelsea Handler, which may or may not get her approval. I might just get sued, and if Snooki sees me in a bar, well let's just say I'll **for sure** notice her first (have you ever *seen* Jersey Shore?? Goodness!) and scram out the backdoor. No shame! That's a lot of difficult and unnerving junk I had to get thru! I'm also learning to follow a little game plan that it seems like another famous comic whom I adore adheres too, and that's Kathy Griffin's noticeable rule of asking permission and then doing it regardless of the answer. Nobody's really gonna give you permission for most things YOU want anyway (*people only care about their own agenda, for the most part*), so sometimes you just have to create a new set of rules for what you want to accomplish.

Let me tell you what I know for sure: **nobody gets anywhere if they**

don't GO FOR IT at some point.

Now I won't go into *how* I tracked these people down, other than you have to be resourceful. People know people who know people, and eventually if you dig deep enough, you'll find an avenue. You can go to www.ContactAnyCelebrity.com, but you'll mostly get Agents and Managers email addys and stuff. (*That's not a bad place to start, but I didn't have a lot of luck there. You might do way better.*) Instead I wanted to get right to the source, so I was very Sherlock Holmes about it all.

Ground Rules: BE UBER POLITE AND NOT STALKER-ISH. Be respectful of their time, and make it short, whatever you want to say (3 paragraphs max!). Use your manners. Have **ZERO EXPECTATIONS** of ever hearing from them! Have **ZERO EXPECTATIONS** of the email even going thru to their inbox. Best case scenario, they DO read it and like you/your work. Worst case, they don't. Doesn't matter either way, but still GO FOR IT IN A BIG WAY. *Cuz you just never know...!* Use your manners and your personality. Be controversial, make them laugh, do something besides vanilla beans, toots! Introduce yourself, compliment them (*duh, they're famous and HUMAN JUST LIKE YOU and everyone loves that shit*), pitch whatever you want them to know, and say thanks. Done. Add your contact info and LINKS to your website(s), videos, books, etc... DO NOT SEND ANY ATTACHMENTS! You'll prob get flagged for spam or junk mail. (*If they ever ASK YOU for attachments, send exactly what they ask for. Not more. Not less. Exactly.*) **You'll be super nervous to hit send.** You might feel like a real asshole. It's ok. Send it anyway. Here's how I see it:

WORST-CASE SCENARIO (*any and all are possible*)

Ivanka Trump, the Jenner/Kardashians, etc. think I'm a dick. I won't be invited to all their family functions, parties, and lavish weddings (*anymore... my invite must always get lost in the mail!*). They deleted the emails/messages. They never even saw it. I went to spam and disappeared.

BEST-CASE SCENARIO (*any and all are possible*)

Ivanka Trump and/or the Jenner/Kardashians know for even one fleeting second who I am and what I do. They actually like what I do. They respect my courageous & empowered act regarding my business and professionalism and they don't think I'm a dick at all! They order some of my art. They tell others about me, and those people order paintings. They think I'm hot like Louboutin and decide to become an investor and help build The Painted Laugh empire with me and we all make millions of dollars doing something cool and beneficial in the world! I get invited to all their family functions, parties, and lavish weddings (*again... now they have my new contact info so my invites won't get lost in the mail!*).

To date, nothing great has come from the messages I sent. YET! But nothing bad has happened either.

Remember when I joined that MLM company and made all of zero dollars?? Well, I did get rewarded in a big way, *just not in the form of cold hard cash.* Not only did I start on the super-freeway of personal development, powerful enlightenment, and real-world wisdom, but I met some amazing people I get to call friends. One of them is this smokin' hot chick Sarah Zolecki, who happens to be both changing other people's lives with her spirit, knowledge & mad skillz AND is making a whole ton of money in that MLM Business that I didn't. (She digs it and has a passion for it, and it makes all the difference!) She's amazeballs, for real. **Sarah is a business Mentor, Speaker, and Trainer as well.** She's a community leader and puts most of the world to **serious shame** with the time and money she gives back to our planet. I asked her to impart a piece of her mojo for you, and this is what she has to say:

© Sarah Zolecki

"

Where do I start? It has not been all rosy! I learned everything, I mean EVERYTHING the hard way. (I guess that's the German stubborn side of me.) The last 15 years of building my own business I learned (or was hit over the head) with these 5 simple concepts:

1. Become You

It took me years to "get it." I would look around and try to copy or be these other people. I think about it now and cringe. How ridiculous I must have looked. **Authentic**. What an awesome word.

I live in So. Cal and let me tell you *that* is a rare word. Everyone is trying to out-do each other in every area of their lives and they are straight-up miserable! Flat out, I made a DECISION to be me, the good, the bad and the super ugly! No more worrying if things were perfect (which they never were), no more making sure everyone was happy except me, and no more *what will people think* (they don't give a rip really about what you think, an "aha" moment for me!). Guess what happened? My business quadrupled! Not only were things rocking but, because I was being myself and authentic in everything I did, **it came naturally!** I didn't have to try so hard to grow my business. I was attracting amazing things everyday because of my simple decision to become me! (P.S. Not everyone will like you. You will have haters... Look at it this way, there are people you don't like, right?!?!)

2. Always **Trust** Your Gut

For you over analyzers, this is tough to do. That instinct is in you for a reason! Every single time I didn't trust my gut, it crashed and burned big time. I think I did this like 10 times before I said I have to stop this crazy cycle. Your gut is your internal compass. So, for those of you that have had a hard time making decisions, **you need to listen to your gut**. If you do, the decision making process will be simple, pain free, and you won't waste anymore time in your life. **(Life is way too short anyways.)**

3. **Stretch** - Kick FEAR in the Face (Wonder Woman Style)

Being meek and mild just won't ever help you achieve what you ultimately want. **BOLD** is so the new black! Every famous celebrity and successful entrepreneur has kahunas! I wanted to be that salmon swimming up-stream. People seem to take the "I'll just settle" route. What... a waste of a life! Getting out of my comfort zone in the beginning felt like Gumby. I knew deep down though that **every successful person lives outside his or her comfort zone.** Being a business owner, I knew that in my comfort zone I would never make money. If I lived outside it, **Sky is the Limit baby!** What's my take on fear? Here's my mindset: **Fear is my green light to go. If I am scared, I <u>have</u> to do it!**

4. Grow like a mad (wo)man

This concept has been white hot in my life forever. It's how I'm wired. I know if you are not growing, you are dying. Period. How many times have we run into people and they look the same, talk about the same stuff and nothing (I mean NOTHING!) has changed? And what sucks is you can't even have a great conversation with them... you are totally on a different page. What happened? You grew they didn't. I get so excited about growing... I know, I'm weird like that... I love going through a growth spurt. It's exhilarating!!! I want to become the best I can be! Don't you? We have one life and it's not tomorrow, its right this very second.

5. Work.

Yes- work it girl (goes for guys too)... Put your dues in. Don't fall into the trap so many other people do of *Entitlement*! Don't have the mentality of that person who throws something in the microwave for 60 seconds and freaks out when there are 20 seconds left! Just like how a baby needs 9 months to grow, things in your life need to incubate as well! I am so sick of people wanting everything, but not being willing to do what it takes. When you work hard and produce results, you can then teach it to others, help others. Let one of your truths be to Walk Your Talk. There is no

such thing as a free lunch. Work, work and work.

You can hook up with Sarah here. (Dude, not like that! She's totally married!) She's a Professional Speaker and Business Coach and helps lead thousands of people toward their Business Goals for a fab Financial $$$ FUTURE!

www.sarahzolecki.com   888-689-6754

Twitter @sarahzolecki   http://www.twitter.com/sarahzolecki

Facebook   http://www.facebook.com/becomeyou

TIMING – IT CAN MAKE A DIFFERENCE

A.K.A. "Helllloooooo, Orange County!" (let me explain)

Sometimes you can be Kung-Fu-Panda-Dragon-Warrior Awesome, and you're doing things right, taking little Action Steps each day, honing your Inner Framework and Focus, and still, nothing is happening. Or worse, bad things are happening, *and that's more frustrating than being stuck in traffic, low on petrol, for 2 hours when you can physically SEE your exit ramp… wondering if you're going to have to call your amazing boyfriend for the 2nd time in your young, fresh relationship and tell him you've run out of gas and ask if he come save you…* My point here is to **keep going**, because things are sometimes a matter of **timing**, and it's not really yours I'm talking about so much as the Man (Woman)-With-The-Plan upstairs. The hardest thing to do is have faith and trust, **but it's imperative**. I guarantee those little steps you're taking are leading you to something big big big when the timing in the world is primed.

I refer to timing as "Helllooooo, Orange County!" because I can then slip in the following story just to make everyone laugh, *which is fuel for my fire in life*. Names have been changed because my friend and the mom in this story would kill me and I would never do that to her unless she was a famous Hollywood star and could get me good Press, which she is not and cannot, so I'm saving her the exploitation. (*To be clear, if she was famous I would sooooo name-drop her ass, faster than the Bachelor/Bachelorette turned lame-city.*)

Setting: My son's 6th Birthday Party, an Evening/Nighttime Pool Event

Theme: Pirates, which has no impact on the story whatsoever

Scene: A couple hours into the party, everyone having fun. Kids are all sugared up; Adults have eaten and had a cocktail or two (*or six, depending on whose wife was knocked up and could drive them home*)… Jacuzzi filled with both Kids and Adults, laughing and talking away. Out of nowhere, **and for no known reason or stimulus**, my son's 6 year-old Kindergarten classmate "Jane" stands up out of the water, lifts her bathing suit top up to her neck, and shouts "Helllloooooo, Orange County!" Her mom was directly across from me, with eyes the size of dinner plates and a look only reserved for such an occasion as seeing your little-girl flash for the first time. As "Lucy" whisked her daughter "Jane" away to have a good talkin' to, we all sat dumbfounded in the cuzzi… then burst out laughing. "Jane's" **timing** was impeccable, *which was the only I could manage the story into this book*. Fun tho, wasn't it?!?! And **THAT**, my

friends, is how we single-handedly raised the bar on a 6 year old boy's birthday party around the country. Shalom.

P.S. We don't even live in Orange County, which makes the story even 10, no... maybe a solid 3x funnier.

HEALTH – WELLNESS – ENVIRONMENT (*They also affect your Spidey-Senses!*)

I'm the new hippy. I recycle EVERYTHING and started a compost pile. I'm a semi-snob for organic-as-much-as-possible and I switched every brand possible to those made with all natural ingredients. I'm barefoot and braless a good majority of my days. EXCEPT WHEN I WEAR TOO MUCH MAKE-UP AND STRAP ON THE HIGHEST (AND MOST DELICIOUS) PAIR OF GORGEOUS STILETTOS POSSIBLE, AND FUCKING LOVE IT!!! I'll also throw down a fast-food-happy-meal for my son when necessary and grab those naughty naughty French Fries for me *and not feel even the slightest tingle of guilt about it... those things are freaking divine!* I know so many women like me, us "new hippies." I think it's cool to embrace both aspects of my braless hippy/stiletto vamp lifestyle, because both make me extremely happy. And that's the secret of life, folks:

Find what makes you happy... and do it.

I do want to spread a little love about the Health – Wellness – Environmental benefits of the new hippy lifestyle for one quick minute. I'm not an expert in this, although when I was switching Majors back at ASU (*Go Devils!*) I **was** in Exercise Science for about 4 semesters. I also read books by the experts, and do a lot of my own research. It's pretty basic, really. Put good things in the temple. Put good things on the temple too. Your skin absorbs all those chemicals and poisons just as fast as if you're eating them.

"But *Sonja, I love junk food and it makes me feel good, like a warm hug.*" I know. I understand. But you have to eat right, and you have to make changes in the way you live. You need a TON of good energy for success, and that means you have to consciously eat better, exercise, meditate (*it's just breathing deeply, darling!*), and re-focus. Leafy greens, antioxidants, chlorophyll, spirulina, wheatgrass (**yuck** – I'm not even gonna lie), tons o'water... they're all amazing for you and support the cause. Humans, it turns out, are actually meant to be plant eaters. You'll note our **lack** of paws, claws, and fangs – which are all the natural signs of carnivores. Now I'm not telling you to go full on vegan or anything, **and I still eat some meat**. (*Although I went to 100% organic, and only grass-fed and cage-free on my animal products because it's better for me and* WAY *better for the animals and environment.*) That matters to me. I'm a big-picture-thinker, and I believe you are too! I also cut way back on my meat intake, nearly cut out dairy completely (*Vanilla Almond Milk is the BOMB, yo!*), upped my leafy & dark green intake by about 600% or more everyday, and almost cut out the caffeine and energy drinks completely (*except when getting close to this book's deadline*). I honestly feel lighter, brighter, happier, and healthier because of it.

Later on I'm going to list Kris Carr again as 1 of the really smart Women I think you should know about in the world...she's this super funny and inspiring woman who wrote the book *Crazy Sexy Diet*. You should read it. Everyone should read it.

INTUITION

Mi amigos over at Wikipedia say that **intuition** is the ability to acquire knowledge without interference or the use of reason. The word 'intuition' comes from the Latin word 'intueri', which is often roughly translated as meaning 'to look inside' or 'to contemplate'. Intuition provides us with beliefs that we cannot necessarily justify. For this reason, it has been the subject of study in psychology; the "right brain" is popularly associated with intuitive processes such as aesthetic abilities. Some scientists have contended that intuition is associated with innovation in creative discovery. (Yay!)

Here are my thoughts on the subject: For the most part, you already have the answers. You know right vs. wrong, you know what makes you feel good & happy vs. what makes you feel drained & depressed. You know what to eat and what to avoid. The problem is you talk yourself out of the truth... you talk yourself *away* from your **intuition** (as a defense mechanism). You know why we all shy away from those "right" things?? *Because if we fail at what we really want, want we really believe as our truth, we don't have a lot left in the areas of* *hope*... if we talk ourselves out of the "right" things **and then** fail at other stuff, it's an easier pill to swallow.

Example: I didn't care very much about all those other jobs I had, so it wasn't really that big o' deal to me if I failed at them. *(It wasn't what I really wanted, you see!)* But to fail at being an Artist would've been the W*O*R*S*T! I was **afraid to fail** at what *I really wanted*, so I decided instead to **not** go for it for a loooooong time. My intuition told me every move I was making was **wrong**, but I kept making those wrong moves anyway... If I just ignored those thoughts and feelings – I'd be ok. I'd be ok. I'd be ok. It'll all be ok.... **OR**, I would end up in the Emergency Room in *almost* as much pain as labor and have a little "Come to Jesus" with myself, putting my life on the scariest and BEST journey of

my life!

You know what you **want** to do, what you're **good** at, and what you'd **like to pursue** a little more.

You just have to bravely step forward towards that, and trust your intuition more. Trust

yourself. Be friends! You're going to be hangin' out with yourself for a good long time, hombre. Better make it a healthy relationship full of open communication!

USING YOUR NOODLE - CHEMICALS AND WIRING

Your brain is hard-wired for repetition. If your habit pattern is stress/doubt/fear, the dangerous brain chemical you release most often is Cortisol. Bad shit. Cortisol is now recognized as a contributing factor in brain **shrinkage**.... *(Hmmm, I'll pass on that option, but thanks.)*

Cortisol = anxiety, depression, self-pity, and insomnia

When you make a step in a different direction, **towards feelings of accomplishment and capability**, your brain releases Serotonin. **Yay** for our friend Serotonin!

Serotonin = focus, problem-solving skills, innovation, and better sleep

Your brain literally creates electricity and begins to fire at more optimal levels with increased amounts of Serotonin... the Dr. Feelgood chemical, oh yeah! The more this becomes your repetitive state-of-mind, the deeper this particular habit forms in your basal ganglia. (*My come again??*) Your basal ganglia, which shoots an enormous number of neural signals to affect your future actions & responses. By choosing to relax and do well at a task, you're strengthening the neutron pathways for more success in the future. So put that in your Hookah and ponder it for a while! How are **YOU** wiring **YOUR** brain these days, and more importantly, is it time for a change???

Guess what else, home-slice... Most of the TV shows and Media **purposely** wire our brains for fear, bad choices, and anxiety... it sells, and it creates MORE, which sells more! (*Addiction, violence, and drama, oh my... Toto, we're not in Kansas anymore!*) No one can change the scenario but you, and as you choose to refocus your behavior and actions, most others around you won't. **That's a toughie**, and they just *might* try to persuade YOU not to, too. The brain's usually helpful empathy neurons automatically kick-in to mimic those around us, so it's really important to be conscious and diligent with our thought choices (no matter how unnatural feeling at first). You really have to be strong on this, and you can

definitely do it! Eventually you may even be the leader, the influenc**er**, creating a positive momentum wave for others. And that's cool. (smiling)

I get a ton of great knowledge and brain facts from www.brainleadersandlearners.com.

Know where you're **going**, not so much where you are right now...

where you are right now matters, but not as much as you think.

A GOOD RULE TO FOLLOW:

Write Drunk. Edit Sober.

That's how this book was done. Just kidding. (sort of)

(I'm a little drunk right now... Note: we should prob edit that out in the final... OMG, I'm just kidding!)

I do not get drunk - I get awesome.

This is where we talk about the Business Plan.

Lesson 1: They suck.

Lesson 2: Grab the vodka and pour yourself a stiffy. *

Lesson 3: Not really. But just in case:

Strawberry Peach Sangria

A) Yum.

B) I study Feng Shui, and I like to drink stuff with peaches because they are the "fruit of heaven," "contain properties of immortality," "signify wealth, abundance, and longevity," and "activate fortune for many generations."

C) Strawberries have a ton of antioxidants.

D) If I'm gonna get hammered, I'm going to tell myself the above justifications and enjoy the experience whole-heartedly. **Clink!** (That was me toasting you. I don't say "Cheers" because *everyone* says it, including my old web designer who was a total nightmare and I'll warn you all about him in Chapter 12.) ((I'm going to Clink or High-Five you and other people throughout this book. It's my thing, it's what I do... it makes people smile! ***If you high-five strangers in the street, they all smile.*** Try it sometime!))

Ingredients

- 1 750-ml bottle dry white wine
- 1 1/2 cups Essensia (orange Muscat, a sweet dessert wine)
- 1 1/2 cups sliced strawberries
- 1 cup peach liqueur
- 1 cup vodka
- 3 peaches, each cut into 12 slices
- 1 large orange, cut crosswise into 6 slices
- 1 large lemon, cut crosswise into 6 slices

- 1/4 cup strawberry syrup (optional)
- 3 to 4 cups ice cubes

Preparation

Mix white wine, Essensia, strawberries, peach liqueur, peaches, orange slices, lemon slices, and strawberry syrup in large pitcher, smashing citrus slices slightly. Let stand at room temperature at least 2 hours or chill up to 4 hours. Serve sangria over ice.

*My suggestion is to not actually drink while **writing** your Business Plan, **just before and after**. If you drink during, chances are you'll end up watching E! and find a Keeping Up with the Kardashians marathon, which gets more interesting as you drink and will seriously impede your progress for that day/night. I mean, *hypothetically*, something like that *could* happen.

I want to begin this frank discussion with the fact that it **IS** ok to cry when writing your Business Plan and crunching numbers... and I'm not speaking figuratively here. I mean to actually shed **watery-tears** and at some points **weep loudly and unabashedly**. I also find the more a person passionately loves and believes in what they do, the more this will occur. Note: the more you drink, the more you may cry as well. (Just sayin'.)

I wrote a stellar Business Plan. The numbers work, the product line and price point is vast (to reach a wide range of customers), and there is a full brand in place to build from. The marketing plan is aggressive, and the media attention and emotional impact for clients is a **home-run combination**. Do you know **how many** Capital Investors and Angel Investors/Angel Networks are **salivating** for this kind of opportunity to work with and mentor a small-business into one of the **major retailers of over $5 million in annual revenue**??? *Ohhh, I see so many hands raised.... You! Yes, you right there. The pretty one! What's that you say??* **None**??? *Well, you are correct!* After 8 weeks of blood, sweat, and tears (some tears that could not have passed a sobriety test, but don't worry, I was at home, with E! on...) and meeting with a number of Investors in an Angel Group, and jumping thru hoop after hoop after hoop for them, and being **praised** and **complimented** on the depth and vision with not just my Business Plan, but my **never-before-seen** concept in general, I raised **$0** in funding. Because I am a "Lifestyle" Business, and they're only into "BioMed/BioTech" for the next several years.

(Bartender! Another Peach Sangria, please!) Just kidding. I'm not that

big of a lush. Case in point: I've had the same number of alcoholic beverages this week as sit-ups I've done, which is zero.

So do I regret all those weeks of work I poured into that Business Plan? (And with all exaggeration or sarcasm aside, I mean honestly about 300-400 hours worth of work.) I literally only slept 3 or 4 hours a night, and I'm a hands-on single mom... at the time I was working one of those crappy-jobs-I-wasn't-very-good-at during the day. I spent 10 straight hours a day for 3 solid days of Thanksgiving Weekend on my laptop at my ex-in-laws house, and was only able to dedicate that much time because they entertained and took care of my son for me. (THANKS AGAIN!) XOXO love you guys!

Well, let me first address "regret" in general... I don't have time for regret. It doesn't serve a purpose, change the past, and can really hinder the choices I need to make for the future... Sometimes I make mistakes, and sometimes I do things I wouldn't want, you know, forever etched into my headstone or anything like that... We all do, and we're all human. I know my mistakes are part of the journey. So are yours and everyone else's. So there ya' go: NO REGRETS... *sometimes re-direction??*

Yes, of course! Then forward progress as planned!

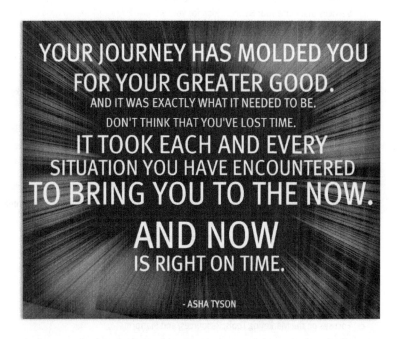

I did NOT get any funding for my business, and that made everything MANY times more difficult. *It threw a real big fucking wrench in the plan, if you really want to know.* BUT, I learned a lot from all those hundreds of hours I poured into my Business Plan. It made me fully invest myself into making this work, and it made me look at numerous aspects of the business I hadn't thought all the way through. It made me put myself out in front of some big scary intimidating people that I **initially** feared. However, I want you to know: you **DO NOT** need a Business Plan to succeed in today's world. You need one if you want to try and get funding (good luck with that as we all know the banks have no soul), and it's *good* to have one because you really do learn a lot. The real deal is you need A PLAN OF ACTION, and most people will think of that as the Business Plan. If someone tells you that you absolutely need a **Traditional** Business Plan, smile and remind yourself that they're thinking traditionally, and you, genius, are thinking Modern Day, **and you have options**. Lemme break some of those down for you:

- TRADITIONAL BUSINESS PLAN (LEFT-BRAIN ORIENTED AND STRUCTURED)
  - **Google** the Parts of a Traditional Business Plan, and start writing!
  - Services that write your Business Plan for you: i.e. www.MasterPlans.com (**Costs** you Money, **Saves** you Time & Head/Heartache, Stress, Hangovers)
  - Doing it on your own (Plan on spending at least 6-8 weeks and about 300 excruciating hours)
    (**Saves** you Money, **Costs** you Time and possible Happiness... unless you like things like this... some people do!) **This is what I did, and I will never do it again.**
  - Needed if you want a Bank Loan, SBA Loan, or Investors (Capital or Angel Investors/Groups)

- NON-TRADIONAL BUSINESS PLAN (RIGHT-BRAIN ORIENTED AND MORE CREATIVE)
  - Books and Coaching Services that can help (i.e. Jennifer Lee www.ArtizenCoaching.com)
  - Doing it on your own (Plan on spending at least 6-8 weeks, but it'll be very creative time spent.)
  - Needed more to understand and focus on your Business needs, goals, and emersion

- NO BUSINESS PLAN, BUT A GREAT MARKETING & ACTION PLAN INSTEAD
  (LIKE YOU'LL FIND IN CHAPTER 12 OF THIS BOOK)
  - Focuses on the Marketing Tools, Resources, and Platforms
  - What's a "Platform"?? (Your Social Media and Circle of Influence... the bigger the better!)

- o Doing it on your own **(Try this one BEFORE that whole fucking Traditional Business Plan above!)**

- COMBINATIONS OF THE ABOVE THREE
(PICK WHAT MAKES SENSE TO YOU AND DO IT)
  - o I found this incredible Mercedes Benz ad, and I just had to put it in here *(it looks way better in color, which is how I originally envisioned having this book printed... Unfortunately, the dolla dollas just couldn't be justified in the end. Bummer. Anywho, you could color it yourself, on the right side in pinks, magenta, reds, orange, green and a little blue and yellow.)*, I love it. I'm a big fan of working with your brain as a whole, so I think if you dissect the parts of a Business Plan and try to brainstorm with the concept of allowing the Right-Brain to contribute to your thought process, no matter how whacky, and then later work out the Left-Brain Analysis, you'll probably have a good handle and clear plan to work from, whether you're going after Investors or Bank Loans, or just figuring out the next logical steps.

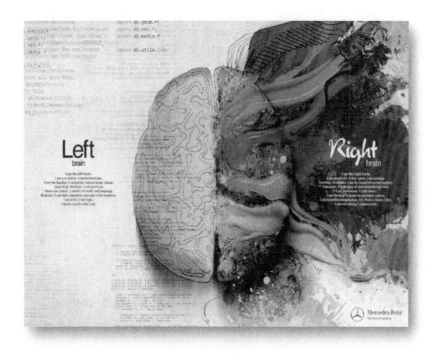

© Mercedes Benz or www.adsoftheworld.com

CAPTION READS:

LEFT BRAIN – I am the left brain. I am a scientist. A mathematician. I love the familiar. I categorize. I am accurate. Linear. Analytical. Strategic. I am practical. Always in control. A master of words and language. Realistic. I calculate equations and play with numbers. I am order. I am logic. I know exactly who I am.

RIGHT BRAIN – I am the right brain. I am creativity. A free spirit. I am passion. Yearning. Sensuality. I am the sound of roaring laughter. I am taste. The feeling of sand beneath bare feet. I am movement. Vivid colors. I am the urge to paint on an empty canvas. I am boundless imagination. Art. Poetry. I sense. I feel. I am everything I <u>wanted</u> to be.

- YOU COULD DO NOTHING, AND NOT MOVE FORWARD WITH YOUR DREAM CAREER **(NOT RECOMMENDED)**

  - Come on, man… Do *something*! This is your **LIFE** we're talking about here! Your mom got heartburn and stretch marks (as the very least of her ailments) to bring you into this world… and she didn't do it so you could slave away in a cubicle or any dead end job headed toward a nice, gray, middle-management ceiling, uninspired and pathetic, wishing you were doing something **else** with your time… **WHAT** ideas are just *dying* inside of you, wanting to come out and make an impression?!?! What is your big creative contribution to the world?? You've got it in there, somewhere! **<u>You do</u>**!!! Yes!!! You!!!

Don't let your small business keep you small-minded.

- Brendon Burchard

CHAPTER **EIGHT:** YOU ARE NOT THE JACKASS WHISPERER – A LOOK AT **FEAR** AND FAILURE

Don't try to win over the haters.

YOU are **not** the Jackass Whisperer.

- I don't know who said this, but I saw it on the internet and it's brilliant

Fear is a very real thing and common reaction to anything new, or big, or out of one's normal comfort zone. There's the fear of failure, fear of being "wrong" or making mistakes, fear of being humiliated, and fear of losing and/or going broke. Fear is directly tied to the ego, and actually acted as a valid indicator of danger back when even ladies had hairy knuckles and their arms would drag on the ground... Since I haven't run in terror from any saber-tooth tigers or wooly mammoths lately, **and I'm assuming you haven't either**, I'd like for us to have a little heart-to-heart about fear and put it in the place it justly deserves in our life in 2011 and beyond. Fear does have a place, but a place we're going to learn to move thru rather than take up permanent residence and buy furniture. I'm telling you don't sign a lease and move-in with fear. (Fear makes for a bad roommate!)

I can tell you **with sincere honesty and experience**, you can make a real ass out of yourself and wake up just fine the next day, breathing in good solid oxygen and putting on cute panties to tackle another 24 hours. I use that knowledge to help me act brave when I'm feeling some fear...

I'll also speak candidly and personally on the subject of going broke. If you're broke, you already know what I'm talking about... Panic, stress, fear, doubt, guilt, few opportunities, few choices for almost anything... (stick with me kid, and I'll show you the way out). If you're not broke, good for you, and try to stay not-broke. Apply your Action Plan to get richer, more fabulous, more fulfilled, and happier, rather than to pull you up from the gutters. Wherever you are today (broke or not-broke), you can make changes for the better and more abundant lifestyle we all crave. (Unless you're a Himalayan monk or something who craves no worldly possessions, in which case I'm humbled and surprised you're reading my book.) So here's my story: I went broke. Not just broke, but brokety-broke-broke and beyond. Several factors contributed to going broke, and I don't regret any of them. One big factor was my divorce. Divorce sucks and is absolutely financially devastating. The thing is, it was still the right choice for us, and now we're friends and work I know for a fact it was my path to go from very comfortable (but unhappy and unhealthy) to broke (but happy and confident) to below broke (not happy and panicking, borrowing a shit-ton of money from people I loved but somehow still confident) to VERY COMFORTABLE AND ABUNDANT (and crazy happy, fulfilled, healthy, energetic, and passionate, living an ass-kicking and generous life built with the things I love most).

Besides the obvious suck-factor in being broke and ruining your credit for a while (*cash is king, plus don't ever let those hoity-toity banks and credit bureaus make you feel less-than when your credit is in the red... they got bail-outs and you and I didn't, so that's that!*), it also isn't the most direct route to self-confidence. I had a near-absurd level of confidence in my success and the success of The Painted Laugh, which got me thru it all but also made the people I owed money to wanna kinda kick me in the teeth at times. I do truly believe though, that God brought me to a place where I could fully understand and fully appreciate what was going to be laid out in front of me with my hard work and His/Her guidance.

Life Lesson: Try not to go broke. Dummy. You could've seriously died out there.

Business Lesson: Try not to go broke. Dummy. You can seriously die out there.

One more thought on "broke-ness" and a little perspective on the entire issue. I was in debt with a garbage credit score, but only "broke" in some very skewed standards. It was hard to make rent some months, and raise my son on only my income, but only in America does "broke" mean you still have a Wii and a cell phone! Because of all the abundance I now have to be exceptionally grateful for, I give generously to those less fortunate than me, and I encourage you to do the same.

I LOVE money! I do! But I'm not emotionally attached to it...

I've been **rich**, driving my Rolls Royce, then bankrupt the next day, taking the bus.

Then **rich** again! I don't care! I'm like, **bring on another day** and I just know it'll be

ok!

- Sharon Osbourne

Time for more Fun Facts and a little perspective on being "poor":

- ✓ If you have food in your fridge, clothes on your back, a roof over your head, and a place to sleep, you are richer than 75% of the world
- ✓ If you have money in the bank, your wallet, and some spare change you are among the top 8% of the world's wealthy
- ✓ If you woke up this morning with more health than illness, you are more blessed than the million people who will not survive this week
- ✓ If you have never experienced the danger of battle, the agony of ramped, daily warfare or terrorism in your community, or the threat of explosives where your

children play, you are luckier than 500 million people alive and suffering

✓ If you can read this message you are more fortunate than 3 billion people in the world who cannot read at all

Alright, so put those fun facts in your pipe & smoke it, and let's keep going on this fear stuff, and equip you to move thru it and onto your greatness. You've got places to be, and it's not stuck in this "fear" chapter too long, that's fo' sheezy.

I've already given you one of the 2 most freeing ideas I've ever heard on the fear of embarrassment/public failure... label it whatever you want. It's the quote on the Jackass Whisperer, because the thing is: not everyone is going to like what you do, and you need to be ok with that. Some people ARE going to like what you do, and that's your ideal client and audience. Don't worry about the others! The second most freeing thing to remember about people is this: they do not care about you and your success or failure as much as they care about their own. It's all relative to their own, all the time. You want proof and an example?? (Demanding! Just kidding, friend!): pictures of stars without make-up in smutty magazines. We'll look and gawk for a second, and then move on and forget the entire thing. However, if it were MY picture in there, I would think about it, linger on it, and give it much more time than the 2.5 seconds worth of attention I gave it before. It's the same with your business and life decisions; it's all based on relativity to THEIR own situation. People really spend very little time thinking about you compared to how much time they spend

thinking about themselves. It's just our human nature to look out for numero uno, and it's also a good way to conquer any of your fears.

Here's the big takeaway. No one cares about your "mistakes" as much as you think. Aside from your mom, who will stay up nights worrying about how bad you are failing while it's happening. (*Sorry mom.*

It's worth it now tho, right?!?! **Love you!** *XOXO*.) People are <u>most likely</u> going to respect you for going for a big dream instead of judging you on mistakes and missteps along the way. I speak the truth!

The point is to be courageous, even when it's scary, because you are up to big things!

A dream you don't fight for

can haunt you the rest of your life, and that's

not one of the experiences I'm signing up for!

In her book, *Bossypants,* **Tina Fey** illustrates the best story of fear, so much so that I actually did LOL. **Tina Fey**, it shall be noted here and now, is hugely talented, funny, and fascinating, and took major kickass-ness steps for women in her industry by becoming the first female head writer for **Saturday Night Live**. This story of fear takes place her first week at SNL. She was brand new, nervous, and had never seen a real movie star up close. The very first host she worked with was **Sylvester Stallone**, and she was required to go to his dressing room and ask him to **enunciate** more just before he was going on stage...

"

... I found myself knocking on the door and being ushered in. Judge Dredd himself was on the couch in an undershirt, smoking another cigar. He looked up at me. I muttered, "In the Rita sketch, you were a little hard to understand. Can you just enunciate a little more?" Stallone was unfazed. "Youcannunnastanme? Youneeme nanaunciate maw? Okay." He couldn't have been more easygoing about it. My guess is that this was not the first time in his career he had been given that note.

I went back outside and manually released my butt cheeks."

Sometimes in life you have to do things that are really hard, and scary, and make you nervous. Do them, and then manually release YOUR butt cheeks, and it'll all work out in the end. (Plus, know that if it's not working out yet, then it's not the end!)

School is in session.

Do you think for one millisecond Snooki cares what I, Sonja Landis, single-mother and Artist in San Diego, California, thinks of her?? Uhhhhh, not even! She's busy buying Gucci and Louis V, making Pistachio commercials, doing Letterman, and building a pickle-inspired flip-flop empire. Which is why I use her in this book. Chick is fearless in her pursuits, even when it's probably been a scary set of choices and actions she's had to make to get there. She also has gotten pretty fit, which certainly shocked the shakira out of me! Then I heard she's writing a 2nd book, no doubt about to be another NY Times Best Seller as painful as that is to admit, about *"How to be a Guid-ette"...* which certainly did NOT shock the shakira out of me.

Do you think Chelsea Handler cares that I'm basing a-frightening-many of my career and business decisions by channeling my Inner-Chelsea?? *WhatWouldChelseaDo??* *WhatWouldChelseaDo???*

The answer, class, to each of these questions is not only "no," but HELLLLLL, NO! Now I'm as human as everyone, and I get all those frozen & fearful feelings too. Fear of failure, fear of judgment, fear of making mistakes and being wrong, fear of losing... But here's the magic: everyone has that same fear, and deep down people respect a person for being brave and taking chances.

Courage is always more commendable than cowardice. Playing it safe **all the time** = lame city! Shake up your dormant courage-skills every once in a while, chica! No one cares about YOUR life/mistakes/insecurities as much as YOU do... get outside of your own little world of fear and think about what you can uniquely & happily offer to others & our planet.

Think of the greater good, not about your own little insecurities (we all have them, and they're like 95% the same for everyone!)

Even after a supreme flop, of which **I've had many**, people sent me messages and told me I had inspired them so much for *trying*, and that they were vicariously living **their own dreams** through me! People were rooting for me to succeed, but also were comforted with all my flops and mistakes along the way. (*No one wants to hear the story of the millionaire who won the lottery... they want the UNDERDOG, man! And Underdog I am!*) People didn't want to watch me walk on Easy Street where it was all rosy and perfect. That pisses people off and discourages them to give it a try themselves. All your fears are normal, and I have them too. So does freaking Oprah. The best way to check your fears is by being authentic and honest; making, admitting and learning from mistakes; re-directing your focus when needed, and consistently moving forward on your path toward

GREATNESS. **Anything** is possible, and don't let anyone tell you different... Can you **imagine** the flack the Wright Brothers got when they said they were going to get man to fly??? OMG! But thank God and honey roasted peanuts they pursued that greatness inside of them!

An old saying goes, "If there's an elephant in the room, introduce it." **Acknowledge your fear.** *(Hi, fear.)* **Recognize you're doing something BIG which feels uncomfortable at first.** *(I'm stretching and learning some new things, fear, and I'm not going to be on the All-Star team right away... and that's* *ok, so you don't have to flare up and over-react, trying to protect me. I want to do this.)* **Go step-by-step and keep your perspective (remember that story of becoming a Doctor??).** *(Today I'm going to take a few steps toward making my kick-ass-life-dreams-and-goals happen. Good things are going to happen slowly, and bad things might occur from time-to-time... it's all part of the process and timing of the Universe, and you can take a load off, fear, because I will be ready for, and be able to rebound from, everything that comes my way.)* **Tackle one action step in your plan.** *(See, fear, that wasn't a big deal! I appreciate your help in stepping aside, and I know you're here for my own good. I know it's part of your job to protect me, and you're doing a good job. I'm not going to ever replace you, but I* AM *going to keep taking these little steps forward and will be asking for more of your cooperation. I'll buy you a drink or something pretty tho in the end. I'm smooth like that. <<wink>>)*

NOTE: This is obviously a verrrrrrryyyy simplified version of coping with fear, but it'll get you started and moving forward... it won't *totally* work long-term. For serious, long-term, and complete understanding/fulfillment with **your life's purpose**, you need to address things on a deeper level. It's no biggie... I had to do it too. It just takes time and skills, and you can find out more on my website **when you're ready.** www.SonjaLandis.com (I have tools, information, and training available for you to use, and I also work with people in Private Coaching sessions to really cut to the chase and get you going on your way. Not everyone is ready at this point, which is why we're just addressing the basic level here and now... For now, I want to get peeps moving and thinking in a forward direction, and those most interested in getting thru the junk can do so when the time is right.)

Here's what I found, and what I learned for sure about MY life purpose as I addressed things on a deeper level of consciousness... it might start to give you more ideas about your own. I am an Artist, and I have Synesthesia, which made me career possible. Synesthesia is an involuntary neurological condition in which 2 senses trigger and cross in my brain. Mine is called Sound-Color, and has been most common historically with famous Music Composers. I actually SEE sound in the air as different colors and patterns. Growing up, I didn't know that others couldn't, so I didn't think much of it. I usually saw the most harsh and unpleasant sounds clearest (clanking dishes, things dropping and breaking), which wasn't exactly a barrel of monkeys. In an awesome and most-welcome twist of fate one day when my son was 3 years old, I saw his laughter in the biggest, most beautiful and vivid Synesthetic experience I've ever had. I was driven to put it to canvas, with the intention of only keeping it for myself. Word started to spread, and more and more parents & grandparents started requesting their own child's laugh... with a lot of innovation and a wicked learning curve in real-world business, my first company, The Painted Laugh, was born. So part of my life's purpose is as an Artist, who sees things others cannot, and is dedicated to creating a beautiful environment for myself and others. I'm also an educator, a navigator, and a leader (all of which have been previous parts of my path) to help others find their true life purpose and then help them succeed at achieving it. That's where this book stemmed from. That's what I'm good at. I make environments beautiful. I do it physically with my Artwork at The Painted Laugh, and I do it with my wisdom and coaching on a person's soul and as they develop their own business and career based on their passion. I also love to laugh, and I use that in all aspects of my life's purpose. I live inspired, and in turn it is part of my life's purpose to inspire others. I was a Navigator in the Air Force where I charted pathways and told others where to go in the fastest and easiest way. When there was a storm, I guided them around it. I then specialized in Electronic Warfare, where I picked up enemy signals and moved good guys out of the bad guy's aim. Do you see the symbolic correlation with those jobs in my past and what I do now?? In business, I connect with really creative and passionate people and chart pathways for success with them/for them. When I work with private clients, I pick up signals they don't often see, and when they are at challenging points (or career changes, or a crossroads in life), I help move them out of harm's way. What is so harmful?? Ummmmmm: stress disorders, unhappiness, unhealthy life choices, a lack of fulfillment in life/career, personal failure and being stuck in fear. (The Center for Disease Prevention (or something like that) in Atlanta estimated that approx. 80% of total healthcare costs in the U.S. are treatments for stress-related disorders/diseases... Big no thanks from me!) I call it The Anti-Gray Suit Campaign; it's the anti-Corporate-drone world. It's all about embracing, empowering, and re-creating the life-force of innovation with the individual Entrepreneur and Small Businesses. It's another HUGE part of my life's purpose: to bust people out of yawns-ville and inspire them to do big things in this world – cuz the world needs more people like you and me doin cool shit and being rewarded financially $$$ for it!

So when you're ready, let's frickin do this thing! www.SonjaLandis.com I'll be super excited to hear from you (when you're ready), sunshine! You'll look better, feel better, and seriously radiate inspired energy and juju from the inside out. Weeeee! XOXO

I **will not** say I failed 1000 times.

I will say that I discovered there are 1000 ways that can cause failure.

-   Thomas Edison

See what good company I share?? Hey, Thomas Edison: Clink! Thanks for electricity, and **not giving up!** Looking for something cool to Google at your sucking-suck-suck job?? Want a little Cliff Claven-esque fun fact to whip out on your friends at parties?? *(Please don't really do that.)* Do a search on who our good buddy Thomas bought the idea that finally worked from… HOW PISSED IS THAT GUY?!?! (I'm not sure if it's true or not, but it's still interesting to know of, right??)

PROCRASTINATION IS FEAR IN DISGUISE

If you find yourself **procrastinating** on things, get to the root of it and I'm sure it's close to one or more of these: <u>fear of failure</u> (*you will ignore that possible outcome and keep putting off whatever you need to do*), <u>a bad story</u> you've been telling yourself ABOUT yourself and now you're living up to it (Work on that Inner Framework and pick one small thing to do each day, come hell or high-water, and promise yourself you will not go to sleep without doing that one small thing. **JUST ONE.** And truly, make it a small thing. Set yourself up for success as much as you can! When I had to tackle my own bad story of procrastination, I decided I was going to walk the dogs around the block – 15 mins tops, depending on how many times the big one, Jake, had to mark his territory – every single day for 30 days. It was good for me, good for them, and good for the creative flow in my work/life.), or <u>lack of energy</u> (*you're not functioning at optimum levels of nutrition, mental/emotional/soulful stimulation, or fitness*).

Brendon Burchard is an expert on this idea of **Efficiency** and **Optimal Levels of Potential**, and I've learned a lot from him. He makes, like, a gazillion-bazillion dollars each year (round-about figure) coaching people to higher levels of **productivity**. He takes **already inspired people** to a whole new level of success. He almost died in a car accident, and when he realized he had been at the steps of the pearly gates and given a 2nd chance, he made a promise to NEVER EVER EVER take it for granted. I definitely think you should check out his work. You can Google "Experts Academy" or "Brendon Burchard" or "Life's Golden Ticket" and you'll find TONS of his stuff. He's really on expert on so many different aspects of business and awesomeness it was hard for me to pick just one. Bottom line: Google him. He makes people's lives better. He made mine better. He'll make yours better too, no matter where you are right now. He also was one that helped me see my responsibility to help others make their lives better with my Lifestyle & Business Advice and Coaching. (Amazeballs, I know.)

"A **hero** is no braver than an ordinary man,

but he is braver five minutes **longer**."

- Ralph Waldo Emerson

Courage is sometimes like breast implants, or a push-up bra: you gotta fake it till you make it, **and that's ok**. *I am a fan of all 3, by the way,* if it gives a girl a little more confidence and gets her onto the bigger and more fantastic issues and endeavors in her life. Own it! Own your courage, even if it's borrowed at first! *Own your boobs too, whether enhanced or au naturrrral.* Clink!

www.wehearttit.com

So I said to **myself**, "Now, I'll just have **to start**

To be twice as careful and **be twice as smart.**

I'll watch out for trouble in front and back sections,

By aiming my eyeballs in different directions.

- Dr. Seuss
I Had Trouble in Getting to Solla Sollew

CHAPTER **NINE:** CHA-CHING

You will be paid in money and dollars $$$ for the amount of **value you bring to other people** in the world. So now that you're getting a clearer picture of **what you would LOVE to get paid to do**, and all the ways you are **unique** in doing so, we just need to develop the system and mentality for actually getting paid to do it... that means, getting it out to more people. (*Ohhhhhhhmygoodlord, I don't want to!* That's your fear talkin', sweetheart. Tell fear to have a seat. You've got good ideas that the world needs to know!)

You've got to **leverage** and **promote yourself** and your work **online**, no exception. You might not be ready this very second to do that (so tell fear to freakin' relax), but we'll get there eventually. You'll be ready when it happens (if my mom, your mom, and all the other moms in the world figured out Facebook and texting, **you'll** be ready and able to figure THIS out). You will be positioned as an expert on whatever it is you love and are passionate about. If you truly dedicate time and focus on **ANY** subject, you will know more that 90% of the people out there, and you really will be an expert.

Example: Snowboarding. I dig the sport, and have been a handful of times, but I literally know nothing about it. If **you** read several articles, blogs, or magazines on snowboarding, did some googleing on consumer products for snowboarding, and had a sincere interest in the sport, you could teach me something. A lot, actually! **That makes you an expert, in my eyes and A LOT of other people's eyes.** There'll be people that know **more than you** on your subject, but there are tons and tons that know far less, and

you can help them. You can become their expert, and you can make money from it. Really. **$$$**
No one will give you the authority to be an expert, but if you authentically position yourself that way, you
can give that authority to yourself, then you can take steps to monitize it. **NO
ONE IS GOING TO DO IT FOR YOU.** Find out what you love and want to do.
Listen to the compliments you get from other people. Put it on the internet using your Step-By-Step Ninja
Guide in the back of this book. **Make money** doing what you love and helping people who are
interested in that same subject. **Win-Win.** Life is good!

You do not need to make it more complicated than that... there are going to be hard parts along the way,
and some stretching outside of your comfort zone, but one step at a time = easy peasy, uncomplicated.

You make **money** online by setting up automated shopping cart(s). Once set up, these run 24/7 and
can reach local, regional, national, and international customers. That's leverage, my friends. That's
power. And that translates into **ca-ching-a-ling-ling** and a trip to Nordstrom with a nice
spa/massage afterwards. It also translates into a lot of great volunteer work you'll have time to do and
the positive impact you can make in your community. It translates into generous time and lifestyle
decisions you can spend with your kids, friends, and family. It translates into a vehicle for you to add
more passions and dreams in your life, to keep growing, and keep doing more good in
the Universe. (All of which beat some crappy "day job" at cubicle-central, right?!?!)

*"But Sonja, my dream is to work with kids, and open up my own daycare center, which is a tradional brick-
and-mortar type of business, and that's what I reallyreallyreallyreallyreally want to do!!!"* No probs,
honeybuns. You're still going to need a website, and innovation, and videos/images
to show parents what a hot-shot facility you have. "Traditional" marketing methods are out out out... and
you'll be with them if you don't boogie on this. Direct mailers get thrown out about 70% of the time
without even being looked at. Yowza. **That's alotta dolla dollas and alotta trees down the tube.**
People spend more time on the internet now than they do even watching
TV. Facebook has 750 MILLION+ users and Twitter as 240 MILLION and counting. Google+ is about to
blow shit right out of the water! You need to get on this fast moving train and I mean like yesterday to
make money doing what you really are passionate about. **You CAN** make your own job, and be
wildly successful, and happy, and avoid anxiety attacks, stress, infertility, and baldness. In fact, **YOU**

SHOULD. As a matter of fact, Mr. & Mrs. Daycare Provider (or any other brick-and-mortar type of business), you can position yourself as an expert daycare facility, an expert with children, and offer some expert knoweldge with one of those aforementioned online shopping carts to either bring you more money and cashflow, or make it FREE with a donation to a charity (optional or mandatory). *"What the hell am I going to sell??"* Your knowledge and answers to problems parents face everyday: behavioral problems, unique learning activities, developmental supplies/toys to enhance the child's environment at home... And if you can't tell me **and the world** you are an expert at what you do, then I wouldn't really want you watching my kid/fixing my leaky pipes/cooking my dinner/painting my house anyways. See what I'm sayin'??

You are passionate about something, and you either have knowledge or want to gain more knowledge on that thing or things. There are **TONS** of other people who are also passionate about that thing or things. Your knowledge is valuable to those other people, and **they will pay you for it**. They will also pay you for your products and services that resonate with it. That is how you build a career and lifestyle based on what you really love, and **it is all possible**. It's not all possible in a day or a week or even a month, but **it is possible with little steps forward**. It is also worth it, and if you believe in and love what you're doing, you'll have your entire life to reap the benefits, leverage your efforts, and continue to grow as a person. That makes for an amazing, abundant, rich life for you and those around you. Enjoy the journey (*parts of it do suck, but let that be the yin to appreciate your yang*). This really is your life, everyday, and your choice to do what you love. This is it, my friend. When it's all said and done, you're not getting another shot. (*At least not in this same body, at this same time, with these same people you love.*) The "shot" you get occurs when you wake up each morning with a new set of choices... it's all up to you what you do with that gift.

You can also make money be being an "affiliate," meaning you offer someone else's stuff on your website, and you get paid some commission back. We have a bunch of affilaites for the work I do as an Artist at The Painted Laugh. www.thepaintedlaugh.com That means more people know about my work, and the people who told them about get 30% of those sales. Win-Win partnerships are created. Friends are made. Good things happen. Can I point out a small affiliate success story to you?? A little company you possibly heard of called Amazon.com became hip to the affiliate concept to the tune of a crazy-staggering 90 Billion dollars. (That was with a "B" and **not** a typo.) Amazon.com didn't come out the gates as a superpower... it started with a guy and a dream, and an idea, and then a website, then a logo, then online shopping carts, a **business** Facebook page, affiliates... just like I'm going to break down for you to follow. Win-Win. *(Can I get an Amen?!?!)*

You can make money online a bunch of other ways. **None of these are my expertise**, and I don't do them... but I know a lot of people who do, and they are making a grip of money! (A good place to start would be **Marc Ostrofesky**'s book *Get Rich, Click!*... he knows all about this and could help you our far more than I could.) You can sell **stuff you don't own yet** on eBay with just a picture of it, then when you make the sale you go buy it and send it out. You can buy domains (like virtual real-estate on the web) and then sell them for profits. You can set up Google Adsense accounts and put other company's advertising on your page, and when someone clicks on it you get like a nickle. Whoopty-doo, I know... but if you're getting a million people a month on your website (and some of the big ballas do!), and maybe 20% of them click on that ad... well hun, I won't do the math right now but it's a lot of nickles coming your direction without you having to do much of anything. Almost free money (remember everything has a price... it'll cost you some time and effort to set it up initially). You can sell books if you want to write, CDs and music MP3s if you're into music, and studded-leather dog collars for pooches if that's your gig. The point is, **you need to do it online now**. We're not moving back in time, and if you're not growing with the internet you're business/career is going to be dying.

Although you can make a lot of money in those ways listed above, the reason I don't do them is because it doesn't really jive with my true purpose, and that's what's most intriguing to me. I attract the clients & entrepreneurs to me and am most fulfilled by working with peeps on the road to their true purpose too. **I want to work with** and am best serving others on this planet by inspiring, coaching, and consulting ultra creative and passionate people who feel the burning desire to live their life all out and make this go-round count. I have the best connections and Media/PR Training and advice for talented, creative types, including Artists, Musicians, Designers, Small Business

Owners, and innovative Entrepreneurs... and usually these people are awesome and already borderline kick-ass at a minimum, so we instantly connect. It's fun to feel those vibes! Wanting to work with these kinds of people also explains why I had the career in the Air Force I did (a *symbol* of my true purpose), but wasn't truly happy or fulfilled... I was on the right track, but still not diving deep enough into the path God intended for me. He/She had more to teach me, more to show me, more for me to learn so that I could pass it on to others. And ohhhh, boy do I ever have some stuff to pass on to you! Weeeeee!

You. Need. A. Website.

Wordpress is the best available with the most flexibility. Plus Google is in kahoots with Wordpress, so it's gonna move you up on the Google Searches, which you want! (I know that's more at the advanced level, but that's why I'm pointing you towards Wordpress.) You can hire a good web designer and get a good-lookin' Wordpress website up for prob $200-$300 and 3-7 days, depending on how intricate you want to get. Another decent option is www.godaddy.com's newer "Website Tonight" option, and you can put something together yourself easily in a few hours. Really. Super easy-cheesy, at least to start you off. It's not the most economical OR the most versatile, but it's better than nothing. You exchange fast & easy for a bit more money. (Remember: you pay the price for everything, and there is NO EXCEPTION.)

You can start a FREE website and blog to get the hang of things and start an online presence at www.Weebly.com and it's about the easiest thing you'll ever do. (Using a round brush and blow dryer at the same time is WAY more complicated that a weebly website.) You can begin by getting it together and getting some of your images and story (About You) on there and not even "publish" it to the internet until you're ready. **Just remember you're not going for perfect!** Perfect doesn't exist and won't ever happen. You're going for authentic and courageous about something you are

PASSIONATE about.

Even if you don't want to "sell" anything online yet, you need to start your web presence. Post some pictures, blog a little bit, set up your Twitter account and Facebook FAN/BUSINESS page. Doesn't matter if nobody "likes" it yet! Who gives a shit! We all start somewhere, and overnight success DOES NOT EXIST. Anyone, doing anything cool, who has anyone that follows what they do, started somewhere. Don't forget that, and don't sell yourself short. **3 GREAT TIPS:** Start right now. A month from now, you're going to wish you already did. 6 months from now, you're *really* gonna wish you already did. A year from now, you're gonna wanna kick your own ass. **So start**. Start. Start! The next thing is (and take it to heart!) even if you're moving slow, you're moving forward faster than the person sitting on the couch, not doing anything at all. Lastly, keep in mind we're all human. You're gonna make mistakes, and want to change things later on, and feel really nervous about putting stuff up on your website/blog at first. That's ok. Just acknowledge it, move thru it, and upload your stuff anyways. Humans like other humans. Humans don't relate to super-humans. Don't pretend you're super-human! Don't wait to BE super-human (ain't gonna happen, lovebug). Both are unrealistic. That equals phoney. **Nobody** likes phoney!

"Sonja, I don't want a website!" I hear ya sister, I was hesitant at first too. And ya know what else?? It's <u>not</u> totally hassle-free or as easy as falling out of bed. It takes some work and some effort. It costs some money, or a lot of your own time and energy, or both. BUT YOU NEED A WEBSITE ANYWAYS. Websites give you leverage. Leverage means you work harder at first in the beginning, and then you work less and less and make more and more money in the end. **You. Want. This.** Leverage gives you drinks on the beach in the summertime at 2 pm on the weekdays. Leverage gives you time, money, travel, and opportunity for you, your family, your kids. Leverage takes you shopping for Jimmy Choos while you're wearing Jimmy Choos. **Leverage = Freedom**. You need and want leverage, which takes work, effort, and time at first. There ain't no free lunch, babe.

What if I told you
10 years from now
your life would be
exactly the same?
Doubt you'd be happy.
So, why are you
afraid of change?

Karen Salmansohn
best selling author of
The Bounce Back Book

www.pinterest.com

PERSPECTIVE SHIFT

Don't get overwhelmed. Instead be thankful for the opportunity to have a lot to do…. It could be worse!
It would be way worse to have not a damn thing worth doing and sit and twittle your thumbs all day.
That's a waste of precious life! Shift your perspective. Whenever I feel overwhelmed, I remind
myself to go one step at a time, have faith, breathe, get creative, move my energy (usually I'll walk the
dogs), and shift my perspective to being grateful instead of stressed. It works most of the time. Drinking
works the other part, so I'm always covered.

TIP: (Given to me by my awesome photographer friend Renee Hindman.
www.reneehindmanphotography.com if you're in the San Diego/Orange County areas. She's amazing!)
Make your website "searchable" at work. I don't know how, but your web designer will. (Or
Google it, I'm sure you'll get directions, it's just I'm not the one to give 'em to you!) I just know you want
to make your website searchable for all the millions of people browsing the stuff they're not supposed to
from their work computer, and you want to make it thru the company's firewall system.

CHAPTER **TEN:** IF SOMETHIN' IS SMOKIN' HOT, HITCH YOUR WAGON TO THAT TRAIN

(An Introduction to "Keywords" and "SEO" – Search Engine Optimization)

I'm not brilliant (contrary to popular belief... *wait, what do you mean you never really thought I was?!?!*). And I'm not particularly lucky. **I am strategic**, and there are definitely 2 reasons I used Chelsea Handler and Reality TV in the title of this book, which is the **Lesson** we're going to discuss here and the 1st reason why they're in the title: If you can tie into something *already* popular, *already* being discussed, and *already* some kind of hot topic, you'll do about 1/100th the amount of work. You're beginning half-way thru the race, and at a fast-pace toward the finish line... and in Business, that's the kind of race you want to run. **And win!** This is all based on keyword research on Google, and a concept called SEO (Search Engine Optimization). **SEO = $$$, if you're doing it correctly AND you've got a good sales conversion and some products/services for sale.** Commit that to your memory as FACT, Jack!

The 2nd reason, is because **I love Chelsea Handler** and good, smutty, voyeuristic Reality TV, and so does the rest of the world. (I also love booze, which is funny, and easy to write about, and why it made it into the title as well.) Most of the world loves each of these things too! So back to my one-sided love affair, minor obsession, and dissection of Chelsea Handler's career plots and rise to fame. I learned a lot, and after watching her sign a 7-figure contract with E!, write several NY Times Bestsellers, and put up her adopted *dog's* profile and getting him 10x more Facebook fans than most people will ever see in their lifetime, I knew I had found my perfect mentor!

REASONS TO ADMIRE CHELSEA HANDLER

- She's not afraid of the truth, and says what's on her mind
- **She doesn't apologize for who she is** or her opinions

- She likes the **Underdogs** (Who doesn't?!?! NOBODY is a fan of "the man" anymore – except maybe "the man") #OccupyWallStreet #OccupyWherever
- She's got, like, the Bad-Girl Oprah Effect on whatever she touches
- She makes fun of herself and can take a joke

- She did **NOT** go to college, but pulls 7 probably 8 figures and gets paid **$$$** to speak at college graduation ceremonies... That's. Fantastic! (You know who else gets paid to speak at Colleges?? Our friend Snooki. I shit you not.)
- She's totally loyal to her friends and **opens doors** for a lot of other people/comedians on her show
- Before she was a hit making oodles and oodles of money, E! had given her a show that was cancelled at the end of the 1st season... but she didn't give up! (She also did a bunch o' junky gigs and TV shows along the way, paying her dues, honing her skillz, perfecting her delivery
- **She goes balls-out in the direction of her dreams**, even when the outlook isn't perfectly rosy
- **She was once super broke, and now she's super rich**
- **She's honest and transparent**, except when she's totally lying, and expects other people to be the same
- She wears full panties with a skirt. (Classy, and I like it!)
- She cusses more than me... (that makes me feel like a Saint!)
- **She's crazy funny**, her timing is genius, and her books are hilarrrr.
- She gets over **7 MILLION** global hits a month, which brings me back to the 1st (and real) Lesson of this Chapter... get in with what's *already* hot hot hot! (Keywords, baby!!!)

KEYWORDS

I used **Keywords** to get higher rankings and more traffic on Google to get more attention for this book, **to sell more books**, to earn **more money**, to buy more stuff that I like & take care of my fam. Not a whole bunch of people knew about this book at first. **ZERO** people were searching for me or my book, and my ego is not too big to tell you that little fun-fact! But guess who people **are** searching for?? My girl Chelsea Handler! So guess how I positioned my book and whose name I used in my video marketing and book title?? Ding ding ding. My girl Chelsea Handler. So now when peeps are searching for Chelsea Handler, guess who's gonna start to *eventually* pop up?? Yep. Yours truly. It doesn't happen right away and my book title would certainly never overtake her being on the top of the searches, but it gives me a humongo burst. That's the power of

Keywords, and I've got a few more tips for you.

- Keywords are HOW your messages/websites/products/services/business gets found online
- Name your stuff after **RELEVANT** stuff people are already looking for when they hit Google... Please make it **relevant** to what you're doing/saying. Be creative, but be relevant! What that means: I found a **creative** way to tie into Chelsea Handler and Reality TV with my book title AND my content (i.e. the chapter you're reading right now)... **Chelsea Handler and Reality TV are actually an important part of the message I'm delivering**. A lot of people search for Victoria's Secret and the GOP, but I don't use those keywords because it wasn't **a part of this book.** If your keywords aren't relevant, it comes across as <u>deceptive</u>, and you're not going to have long-term success based on deceiving people... You'll look like an ass-clown, really.
- Use the Google Keyword Tool for IDEAS and PHRASES people are ALREADY searching... go to Google. Type in Keyword Tool. Follow their directions. It's very easy.
- Videos will get pushed to the top of searches... Google (and PEOPLE!!!) loooooovvvveee videos! Millions of videos get watched **every single day** online. YouTube and videos are making "normal" people into very wealthy superstars every single day. Videos completely level the playing field. You can actually get just as many views for your video online than by going on The Today Show. **Welcome to 2011.** This is what Business looks like now, my friends. And, it bears repeating, videos move to the TOP of those Google searches so more people find out about you. Videos make this happen:

  More People = More Value You Can Deliver = More Money = Happy You = Happy Others

- Use your LOCAL AREA when you figure out your KEYWORDS, **especially** if you serve the local market more than most (i.e. you've got a brick and mortar business you want to get more busine$$ for)

  Example: You live in Colorado Springs and freaking love to golf, and you're not so bad at it. You know a lot about it. You put up a website, nice pics of you on the course or whatevs, some general golf facts and junk... you get the idea. You start to blog a little bit about golfing, courses, funny caddy stories, new clubs and products you like, etc... You want to start getting paid for Private Lessons, and you shoot a little video. You introduce yourself, talk about the Private Lessons thing and give your contact info, and use relevant keywords to tag your video, such as: "Colorado

Springs Golf Pro, Colorado Springs Golf Lessons, Colorado Springs Golfing, Colorado Springs Golfers, Colorado Springs Golf Courses, Private Golf Lessons Colorado Springs, Garden of the Gods Golf, Garden of the Gods Golfing"…. Etc. Here's why: Right now, you're target market is Colorado Springs, not Tampa or Phoenix or anywhere else on God's Green Earth. You're also going to have less competition if your keywords are for your specific area, so you'll come up higher on Google. (Less competition = higher rankings for your stuff.)

"Sonja, I don't know what the fuck any of that means. I hate you." I know, dreamboat… **it feels like that at first**. Your best bet is to set up a website and YouTube channel for whatever your dream career is or however you want to make money… For example, I want to sell this book. **Keywords** I'm using include: Chelsea Handler Book Review, Chelsea Handler Fake Book Review, Chelsea Lately Book, Chelsea Handler Book, Reality TV Book Review, Reality TV Video, Masters Degree, Get a Masters Degree, etc… I use these **Keywords** throughout my website and to **describe the VIDEOS** I put up on my YouTube Channel. Then when people Google Chelsea Handler type stuff, eventually my book starts to surface, and more and more people find out about what a sweet book I've written. More people buy it, and the Media starts to get a little buzz… Viola. I'm making money, selling books, and inspiring more people to do the things they REALLY want to do in life. I'm using relevant **Keywords** to spread my message faster and farther than I could on my own. Leverage. Smile.

What's the deal with Reality TV??

I'm glad you asked! "Reality TV" simultaneously goes along with the Keyword strategy while pretty much overtaking our culture and living rooms. How come?? Because it's a train wreck, and just like our friend Snooki, we all love train wrecks! Including me! (You think I don't DVR that shit, you better think again!) Do I feel the brain cells draining as I watch it?? Sure. It's escape-ism, and more than regular scripted TV, it brings the everyday idiots and assholes front and center, and if they can do it, we can do it. The people aren't perfect, beautiful, and certainly not classically trained! There's no Julliard goin' on with the Reality TV, and that makes it all the more **relatable**. It levels that playing field! It lowers the bar. It sometimes takes the bar away completely, as in The Real Housewives of Atlanta. (Even I have to draw the line somewhere, and TRHOA doesn't make the cut. I can only take *so much* asinine behavior… seriously.)

VIDEO MARKETING

One more time with the videos... You know what else levels the playing field?? Those videos on the Internet! (*Not the sexy ones... go ahead and keep those to yourself.*) Videos on the Internet can spread like wildfire (especially with hot keywords!), allow you to **personally connect** with thousands of people without actually meeting them, and (when done in a nice, professional manner) quickly establish you as an authority figure or expert in your field. Positioning... memba that?? Well, here it is again! *"But Sonja, I hate how I look & sound on video, I don't know where to start, I don't know what to say, and I absolutely don't want to do no videos, no way, and no how!"* Believe me, I had a big block against this too. **I felt like an idiot** at first in front of my **own** Flipcam, yet I was trying to get booked on Oprah and The Today Show... hmmm, well that's not gonna fly at all. How was I going to do National TV when I couldn't even flipcam in my own house?? You've got to get over it. I've got some tips, and the best thing I can tell you is just to start. You can edit the videos, and the more you do, the better you get... They even become fun after a while. Don't be perfect. Don't be too slick. **Be yourself.** Be natural, and just do it. People are going to like you for being you: being transparent, telling the truth, and having a **natural conversation** – who you are, what you do, and why you love it.

There's a sick website www.TrafficGeyser.com where the co-founder, Mike Koenigs, teaches really in-depth Video Marketing techniques, and provides a service to populate them quickly & easily on the Internet. It takes time, and effort. It's NOT going to be automatic. **It takes your action, but it's not hard!** You can try it for $1 for 21 days, learn a TON of great info and put videos out, and then either cancel your membership or pay $97/month to continue to put your videos out all over the net. (It's totally worth it tho... He teaches you everything you need to know and provides what you need to do it. **I don't know this dude, and I don't get paid one penny for telling you to go there. I just know I use it and it works.** According to Mike/Traffic Geyser There are an estimated 1 BILLION web users watching videos EVERYDAY. 60% of Internet use is web videos now... That's a lot of potential customers waiting for you!)

- Introduce yourself. *Hey, I'm Sonja Landis, Artist and Founder of The Painted Laugh Studio and Author of the book, "My Master's Degree is Useless?!? How Chelsea Handler, Booze, and Reality TV Teach Better Modern-Day Business Lessons Better Than The Lecture Halls." It's a really funny business book unlike any other ever written. I encourage cussing and drinking alcohol, even providing some amazing Sangria recipes I love and hope you'll love too. I help Artists, Writers, Small Business Owners and other really creative Entrepreneurs package and promote* themselves **so that** they can get THEIR work, message, and name out there in a bigger way so they can make MONEY doing what they actually LOVE, and I do it by making people laugh and really think about their life and career in a whole new way.

- # Invite them to find out more info, and where. (You can offer them more FREE info too!) *I try to make people laugh, and teach them effective, Modern-Day business practices to get paid more money in their careers. If you want a sneak peak at a Chapter or 2 in my book, get it here: www.sonjalandis.com. It's also on Amazon.com! (Capture their email address to add to your list, Traffic Geyser teaches you how to do it really easy.)*

- You can also: Teach them something, or do a Product Review of something helpful in your specific expertise. Answer some FAQs (Frequently Asked Questions) that people ask you all the time. Be entertaining. Tell your story... Just start to interact, and the **right** people will be interested and start to find you. You will attract the right clients, and your "work" becomes more lucrative, fun, and leveraged.

- # Keep putting videos out there! You can't just do one or two... you have to **continue** interacting and building relationships with the people who will pay you for what you do or know. **Be authentic**, and receive the money and lifestyle **you deserve** because of it.

- Your videos should be professional, but not "slick" like some corporate advertisement. People respond more to real people than anything else. The best ones are between 1-3 minutes. Look nice. Have some good lighting... mine is never the best, but it works ok... I literally just use house lamps... Hollywood movie set it is not; cheap, quick and easy it is! That works for me. I'm not looking for an Oscar Nom for Chrissssssake! Rules apply like your glamour headshots: plain (or nice) background that is either neutral OR supports your message...

  Trainer + Gym = makes sense

  Artist + Studio/Artwork = makes sense

  Chef + Kitchen = makes sense

  anyone + plain background or nice setting = makes sense

  anyone + beach/nature = makes sense AND good natural light

- In your videos, **you** get to dictate what you're putting into the world. No boss, no rules. It's just you, telling your story. You're in total control. I know it's outside of your comfort zone at first, but just start it and give it a try. Keep some perspective: have you seen the best Actor's audition tapes and B movies when they were younger and starting out?? Garbage! The difference is they kept going, learning, stretching... and it all gets easier. If Snooki can do it, you NEED to do it. Grab a Flipcam or little Kodak zi8 or just use your webcam. Small steps, sugar!

CORPORATE SPONSORSHIPS & NON-PROFITS

Last thing to get you in the fast-lane on the money track. If you can hook-up with Corporations and/or Non-Profit Organizations who share the same message as you, pitch them! You can offer them a solution to their problems, and that's how you present yourself/your business. THEY ARE ALREADY CONSTANTLY TRYING TO MARKET TO THE IDEAL AUDIENCE... IF YOU HAVE THE SAME AUDIENCE, YOU CAN HELP THEM (while helping yourself, and they totally know that... they're in business same as you, so don't even think twice about it!). YOU ARE **NOT** COMPETITION. YOU ARE A **COLLABORATOR**!

You can offer new experiences to their audience that they've never had before and can't have without you. You can relate to the audience and help the big, bad Corporations get their products/marketing directly in the hands of the people. **You are "the people"!** For Non-Profits, you can donate your work/time to get new money flowing their way, and they'll have thousands and thousands of people on their list who will find out about **your** work. With www.thepaintedlaugh.com I pitched Crayola and got them to promote my work on their Facebook page (of over 250,000 people) AND offered their list a special DISCOUNT CODE for anything on my site. If people like Painted Laughter, they get a great experience and save money *because of Crayola*! So people love Crayola more, and now like what I do too! **Win-Win**.

For Non-Profits, I've donated sooooo much of my Artwork to different Children's Foundations. It **costs** me some money and A LOT of my time, but the **benefits come back to me** with more people finding out about my Art, and my work going to a good cause (like raising money in a Cystic Fibrosis Foundation Auction). **Win-Win**. See the theme here? Tons of new potential clients exposed to you/your work, and a WINNING (#charliesheen) situation for them in some way. It's not without a lot of effort and time on your part... plus probably like 1 in 25 Companies/Non-Profits will even really respond to you (be prepared for that), but when you finally do get the "**yes,**" you've moved into the fast lane!

Brendon Burchard, I mentioned him before, is really a great person to learn from. He teaches a program on Sponsorship Marketing... it's pricey, but really valuable in content. (Everything I did, I did on my own. It **cost** me a lot of time and energy, but didn't cost me a lot of money. That was my choice. If you have the resource$, you might want to go thru his program and get, like, the PhD of Sponsorship Marketing skills.) You can find out about it here: www.ExpertsAcademy.com

CHAPTER **ELEVEN:** FAME AND FREAKIN' FORTUNE – YOUR NAME IN LIGHTS

"My personality just does not work without fame. Without fame, this haircut looks like mental illness."

Alright, so maybe you DON'T want to be famous. **I get that.** I don't particularly want to be ridiculously famous either, stalked and photographed when I'm eating and grocery shopping with no make-up on or beach-frolicking with any (*or every*, unfortunately... let's be honest & serious) cellulite dimple rippling in the unfiltered natural sunlight... But I **DO** want to be moderately famous, and so should you. Here's why:

In our country and society, famous people have social powers to influence and a level of perceived authority... even when it's unfounded. Lindsay Lohan is still getting paid (albeit pretty poorly, relatively speaking to her peers) to advertise shit. That's silly, I know, but it's true. Press and Media, even local stuff, gives **YOU** a certain level of instant credibility and confidence about your message and contribution, and it feels good! It's not about puffing up your ego... **it's about being able to reach a bigger audience/more clients to sprinkle your excellent mojo on. You are a benefit to the planet if you're getting more attention for doing amazing things in the world.** (You are a drain to the planet if you're getting attention as a self-absorbed a-hole.) DO NOT tie the idea of Press & Media to only Celebrities or <gulp!> Reality TV stars and their lunacy... instead accept it as leverage to quickly and efficiently reach more, do more, benefit more, and inspire more. That's a great thing! And you'll make a ton more money, another plus!

Oh, and if you **DO** want to be insanely famous and stalked by TMZ, I say **go for it!** *Try not to end up doing blow off of people's body parts or Snooki-fying yourself.* Remember: Press and Media attention is about furthering that **LEGACY** you're proudly building with your unique contribution and talents... neither one would benefit from blow. Or Snooki.

PUBLICITY BASICS

- Be natural
    - Speak clearly
    - Shoot videos of yourself (*not the nudies!*) and watch your speech/mannerisms – this is **the best**, *most horrifying* yet helpful, media training you can get... and it's FREE! Study your body language and facial language, and get used to being in front of a camera
    - Be yourself – if you try to be someone you're not you'll be much more nervous
    - Practice – Be able to show/talk (or cook/talk) at the same time (it's not as easy as it sounds)
- Be credible
    - SPELLCHECK your email correspondence, including the Subject Line... first impressions always last! (I'm realllly bad at remembering to Spellcheck. Prob about 30% of my emails and blog posts and stuff go out without the Spellcheck... aghhhhh! It's a terrible feeling.)
    - Know your material

- o Have a tie to timely newsworthy events – Be CREATIVE about this!
- o Know the outline/format of THEIR shows/magazine/etc…
- Be likeable
  - o Be polite, patient, and persistent with following-up… these guys are slammin' busy, and sometimes it's a matter of timing (it's ok to get a "no thanks" or no response at first!)
  - o Good personality with a good story – Why are YOU unique and special??
  - o Have a "Here's what I can do for YOU (and YOUR AUDIENCE) attitude"
- Is your product, service, or cause something **their audience** will get behind and relate to?
  - o Mass appeal/concern… Get statistics if that could pertain to your show idea
  - o Is there controversy involved?? *Peeps love them some drama!*
  - o Are you solving people's problems??
  - o They ONLY care about the angle/segment – NOT you/your products – look for a good ANGLE AND STORY SEGMENT FOR THEM (which *happens* to correspond with you/your products in the end)
- Can **YOU** convey that message in a compelling way for the audience?
  - o Create "Hooks" and include 5 Talking Points for different angles
  - o "Hooks" need to be controversial, solve a widespread problem, or create *FEAR* in the audience… yes, fear! Because like I've already pointed out – the Media LOVES to sell FEAR to people!
  - o What SHOULD people know (that you can tell them) to make their life/family/pets/health better?
  - o Develop relationships with the Media/Producers and brainstorm ideas together – Be a collaborator to HELP them come up with great ideas/experiences their audience will LOVE
  - o Come from a spirit of service, excellence, and distinction
- Misc Helpful Tips (Outlined further in your Ninja Action Plan, Chapter 12)
  - o **NO ATTACHMENTS ON EMAILS!** Most big shows/magazines/companies have super-high spam filters set, and sometimes anything with an attachment gets automatically deleted (links are ok)
  - o Speak in a 10-15 second, condensed manner… This is called a "sound byte"
  - o Have a 2 minute video up of yourself on your website (and send them the LINK to it) because the producers are going to want to see you on camera and hear your voice
  - o **Have a "Press Kit" available on your website,** and have it available in pdf form to email out IF they request it. A Press Kit consists of a "One Sheet" (which includes your glamour shot, super condensed version of your bio, YOUR CONTACT INFO, PHONE NUMBER, EMAIL, AND WEBSITE, and 5-7 bullet points of show/story ideas for THE AUDIENCE'S BENEFIT or timely news tie-ins); any Press Releases (Google how to write it, and follow the examples you find); any previous Press/Media/Experience/Letters of Recommendation FROM those sources (not from your mom and your neighbor). Oh yeah, and make that glam shot semi-current, like within 5-10 years (if you Botox)… you need to be

true in your representation. Same goes for dating sites, but that's really not what we're focusing on in this book...

o If you're local or can travel quickly (or can Skype or something) let the Producers know you are available on short-notice and if they're ever in a pinch, they should call YOU! (This goes back to that idea of how YOU can help THEM make a good show segment.)

I have a lot of funny friends, and one of the 2 funniest (it's such a close tie, I can't pick between them) is my friend **Brandon C**. He is at the center of every party, mix, and happenin' event you can think of, and works at one of those super high-end Beverly Hills PR Firms with the hoitiest-of-the-toitiest clientele. **Brandon** is a PR genius, and was the Media Consultant and Right-Hand Man of **Steve Wynn** for a number of years before being lured (meaning kidnapped, drugged and bound) to the City of Angels. (**THE** Steve Wynn, as in owns half of Las Vegas Steve Wynn.) So Brandon knows a thing or ten about Publicity and the Media, and I've learned a lot of those Press and Media tips from him, among others.

If you're ready to tackle this on your own and get started, you can also Google both Steve Harrison for some Press and Media Magic (he's expensive but REALLY INTELLIGENT), as well as a website called **"Help A Reporter Out"** where you can create a FREE account and be alerted for all kinds of Media outlets looking for people in tons of different categories for the stories they're working on at the moment. They are literally REQUESTING to be contacted and pitched about YOU and what YOU DO.

(If you totally miss this reference you *might be*, nope, you probably ARE over 30. That's ok.
It's not a big deal.)

When they say "no", and they will. A lot. The **#1 Question** to ask:

What *could* I have said

(or done)

to make that "no" a YES?

\- Jack Canfield

Author of the minutely popular *Chicken Soup for the Soul* series, probably about 837 different
versions/types by now…

Getting feedback to that particular question will help prepare you for the next time you pitch an idea to them, or to another show. It's a constant learning experience, and the key is to always be polite and keep building that REALTIONSHIP with the Media so when the timing is right, YOU are the person on the top of their list to call.

If someone tells you "no,"

you're *just* talking to the **WRONG** person.

\- Kris Jenner (Kardashian)

<u>Never</u> let the fear of striking out get in your way.

\- Babe Ruth

CHAPTER **TWELVE:** YOUR STEP-BY-STEP GUIDE TO NINJA SKILLS AND ACTION

DON'T *WISH* FOR IT. **WORK FOR IT.**

Before we start your **Ninja Guide** to Action, I want to talk about this picture quick. It's a gladiola (which are my faves and remind me of my Uncle Jack), and **if** it was buried deep enough, watered, and weeded it would have a nice life... (*I apologize to the gladiolas and every other plant/flower I will tend to in my life. You can note my lack of green thumb here.*) Also, **if** this gladiola was not in a place where my son's enormous exercise ball that he and the neighborhood kids like to play "Wipeout" (like the game show) with on our trampoline didn't smash it on a daily basis, it would be standing tall and in bloom, despite the semi-embarrassing gardening skills already noted.

If, if, if... this flower says, "eff all your ifs!"

Watch me bloom, anyways! That makes me smile so much!

Instead of saying *"but its bent!"*, **marvel that it's in bloom and still reaching up** like it's supposed to. Instead of looking at what shitty circumstances this flower is in and the weeds I need to pull, **notice that it's flowering anyway**. Instead of focusing on the leaves on the ground, **reflect on the effort** this little guy is giving me... he turned out to be a bright orangey-yellow, by the by...

No matter the circumstances, no matter how many times a giant exercise ball lands on YOUR head in life, keep growing, keep reaching up, keep blooming.

I'm doing it too, everyday, thru the goods and bads!!!

I'm also hiring a landscaper. (Clearly, I need one. Know thyself!)

Alright Ninja, let's start your plan...

www.google.com... Search images for "chick ninjas"

To **climb** a steep mountain requires a slow pace at first.

-William Shakespeare

She turned her can'ts into cans,
and her dreams into plans.

➤ 1. YOU NEED TO KNOW WHAT YOU **WANT** TO DO

Make those lists of what you're good at, what other people compliment you on, and what you want to learn more about. Be creative and give yourself permission to want what you want and don't feel any guilt about "why" you want it.

Who gives a rat's ass why you want it? You just **want it**, and that's all that matters. I want to be an Artist. I want to live in San Diego, California and be active outside all year round. I want to feel truly happy, healthy, balanced and fulfilled. I want to work as a Business Consultant and Lifestyle/Career Alignment Coach and help other people get out of their ruts, frustrated, and overwhelmed places. I wanted to write this book. I want to make people laugh... See?!?! (It doesn't matter *why* I want these things – I actually don't know, and think the energy required to figure out the *why* is focused time & effort I can be using to pursue those wants instead of analyzing and dissecting them.) I want what I want in this life because it's deep inside of me, brings me pleasure, allows for lifestyle/career/family/passion **balance and alignment** in my soul. It just is what it is. It's just what I want, and I'm allowed to want what I want. **So are you!** So go ahead and want what you want! I think you know what that is, if you just listen to your own voice!

www.google.com

➤ 2. YOU NEED A WEBSITE

Please oh please oh please, CHECK REFERENCES. I got burned and partially sub-merged, nearly sunk, because I got betrayed and strung-along by my very first "professional" web-designer. He was a snake and a liar, he talked a good game, and I didn't properly check references. That was my bad, and it **cost** me a LOT of time, money, and opportunity. It also made me look unprofessional with his junk website, and that probably irritated me the most. To that dude, and you know who you are, I still feel this way, a little bit:

www.pinterest.com

Buuuuuuut, here's the great thing, and why I believe in no regrets and using mistakes as a learning tool: I interviewed web-designers differently, as did everyone I was in immediate contact with (*so I kinda and inadvertently "took one for the team" if you will*), and I ended up finding the greatest, most polite, professional, respectful, honest, and time-conscientious NEW web-designer, and we've collaborated on more and more projects together to create a lot of

awesomeness. He brought my Rock The Painted Laugh Digital Mic™
from my concept & ideas to reality & functionality. He's super smart in all the places I am not, and
I will be forever grateful to have found him right after that idiot douche bag I had first worked
with. The new guy flawlessly swooped in and saved the day, like Superman. (*I've never seen him in
tights, but he just might be able to pull it off...*) Anyways, to the **good** web-designers out there,

<h2 style="text-align:center"><u>especially mine</u>, Clink!</h2>

www.ffffound.com

Just take one step at a time. This isn't a sprint.
It's also not the end... things evolve and change. I'm still learning myself, and always adding more!
(But this is a great start and will keep you busy for a while!)

Steps to get a Website:

1. Think of a name for your website. Easy to spell. Easy to remember. Easy to pronounce. Relevant to you/your stuff. Not too long. Use common sense, guys & dolls...

2. Go to www.godaddy.com (or any other **domain registration** site) and register the name you picked for $10 for the year. Only get the **"dot com"** for now. Skip all the other stuff they try to offer you, except maybe the email. I think that's a good thing. I like having sonja@thepaintedlaugh.com and feel more professional using that than a Gmail domain. If what you want is taken, return to Step 1 and start over. Continue this cycle as necessary. WRITE DOWN YOUR LOG-INS AND PASSWORDS IN ONE PLACE.

3. Get a FREE Facebook BUSINESS or "FAN" PAGE that matches your new domain, and a www.twitter.com account. You can do Google+, Yelp, YouTube, LinkedIn, BlogFrog, etc... there are a gazillion Social Media sites, "bookmarking" sites (I don't even know or

care exactly what that means), and you want as many as you can with kinda the same images and themes. WRITE DOWN ALL THOSE PASSWORDS IN THAT ONE PLACE AGAIN.

4. Go to www.hostgator.com (or any other **web hosting** site) and set that up for like $12/month or something... *I don't really know so don't quote me on that.* Yes, you can get web hosting at godaddy... I think it's a couple dollars more/month but it saves you some time and keeps everything organized and together. ADD YOUR LOG-IN AND PASSWORD TO THAT ONE PLACE I TOLD YOU TO USE FROM BEFORE. THIS IS CRITICAL. IT IS MOTHERF#@*ING FRUSTRATING TO LOSE YOUR PASSWORDS TO YOUR SHIT. DON'T DO IT!

5. **Hire a web designer** from Craigslist (check referrals and their portfolio) or ask friends of yours **with websites** for referrals. (*You can learn how to do put everything together yourself too, but for me, it's $200 well spent to have someone else do what I want in a couple days than for me to fumble with it for hours, days, weeks, months... If you want to figure it out yourself, do it. High-five. I have no tips for you, except to go to wordpress.ORG and **NOT** .com. I heard it's because .com isn't supposed to be used to make money, and we want you to make boat loads of scrilla. I hear if the free .com site finds you making money they can shut your website off. That would blow.*) Have web designer give you a nice, simple logo too. You don't need to get super crazy ridiculous at this point. Just clean and professional-looking. Here was the exact post I had on Craigslist (**after** lessons learned from web designer disaster #1). I found several talented people to meet with face-to-face before deciding on my first-round-draft-pick Lucas. (It doesn't hurt that Lucas looks like Zac Efron, and I'm not kidding in the least bit. He really got hired though because he was super talented and could add **the most** to my project needs, and that's the real deal! $$$!)

MY SAN DIEGO CRAIGSLIST POST, MAY 2011:

Header: Wordpress Intern/Short Term Position!

You are NEEDED for a very creative project/web design. Pay is TBD. SEO ideas/strategies greatly appreciated and rewarded, perfect for your portfolio. Sense of humor a big plus. We're no stiffs over here... we've got big, imaginative ideas and great taste, just not much tech savvy.

If you're ridiculously good looking but not funny, please email us anyways and we'll make the exception.

We're just kidding about all of that, honestly. If you're still reading this you just might be our guy/chick for the job. Holla! ***PLEASE no agencies, firms, overseas developers, phonies, people that are going to just outsource, or project managers with a staff of developers. We won't reply if that is the case. We're looking for an Independent Programmer and really good, HONEST person that can help. No a-holes please. Thanks.

And guess what that ad got me?? The perfect web-guy!

- Give your web designer your passwords, any ideas you have, any websites you really like, and tell them you need a logo, a blog, an "about" page, a shopping cart, "pages" for any relevant content specific to what you do, and tell them you want all your Social Media sites linked. Send your web guy/girl your super-hot professional headshot(s) and other images and content (written stuff) you want your website to say. My writing voice is very, ummmm, **distinct** (if you could not already tell!) and I wanted my website to reflect that as much as possible, so I had to write the majority of my own stuff. You CAN hire it out; it'll cost you some extra dough.

6. **Check out this Bartlett Pear Sangria recipe I found in Cosmo cuz that was a lot of work…**

    2 diced Bartlett pears, 10 lemon slices, 1 bottle of pinot grigio, 1 cup triple sec

    1 cup brandy, Ginger Ale, mint for garnish (optional)

www.cosmopiltan.com

    Combine all ingredients in a large bowl. Let it sit for at least four hours. (*shhhhyeah, right!*) When serving, ladle the sangria into an ice-filled glass, and top with Ginger Ale. Garnish each glass with a sprig of mint. (*I think I will, thank you!*)

    Source: Fiamma Trattoria, The James Hotel, Scottsdale, AZ via www.Cosmopolitan.com "Meet Your New Favorite Cocktails" (*Hello, cocktails!*)

REWARD YOURSELF ALONG THE WAY FOR THE STEPS YOU TAKE. If not in awesome Sangria recipes, than your reward can be as simple as acknowledging yourself for the work you're doing! Try saying this when you look in the mirror: *"Good job, hot shit! You're moving forward and getting some work done. Life is so good, and they say you are what you eat, but I do NOT remember eating a sexy beast! Rawrrr. Keep going and smile more! You look so beautiful when you smile! Love you!"*

7. Understand your web guy/girl. This is their job. **Respect them, their time, and their craft.**

   - Expect to pay between $20/hr and $100/hr for their time. An initial wordpress website should only cost you about $200 - $500 MAX. If they're quoting too high, keep looking. Run your post again and you'll find the right person. (Unless you have an intricate and detailed web design and needs, like mine was for www.thepaintedlaugh.com. I paid a lot more for that site, but I needed a lot more done.)
   - Expect them to need some things from you along the way: input, ideas, images, content (written part), etc.
   - Expect them to take several days or more, depending on how intricate your ideas are. (*They aren't Jesus Christ in the flesh, and you're probably not their only client.*) Also, no matter how awesome they are (LUCAS!), expect some delays, bugs, changes, mistakes. Roll with it. Revisit a Sangria recipe if necessary.

   However, the good ones will keep you in the loop and not get ridiculous about delays. (*That first idiot said it would take him 16 business days and 12 WEEKS later I still didn't have a website. That's why I sued his ass and won*). **REMEMBER 2 THINGS: You're the boss. We're all human.** Balance those. Be ready for delays/changes/questions/clarifications but don't let a web designer act like a lazy dick either. Trust your gut. Be reasonable & respectful and expect the same thing in return AT ALL TIMES.

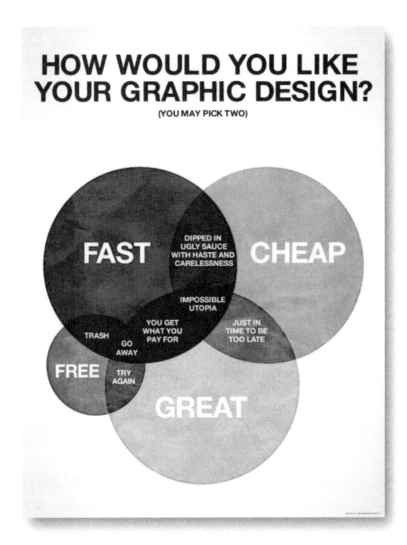

*NOTE: You can go to www.weebly.com, www.godaddy.com, or www.web.com and set up your own website without a web designer or having to code anything. Of all of them I like the creativity of Weebly best, but GoDaddy has 24/7 phone support. It's totally up to you. There's also VistaPrint, but I had a LOT of customer service issues, hassles, and basic jack-assery when I needed to switch from them to my custom-built site... I will never work with them again, but it's an option available for you to check out if interested. The cool thing with VistaPrint is that you can easily order matching business cards, flyers, and other offline Marketing materials you might eventually want.

➢ YOU NEED TO LEARN SOME INTERNET STUFF, but just take your time

- O Set up an "Auto-responder"
  - ▪ You can Google around for it, but I would say most people use www.AWeber.com (that's what I use, and it's easy) or www.MailChimp.com... There are bunches of them, so just pick one and start learning how to do it.
  - ▪ Your web designer might know how to do this for you and have his/her professional suggestions. If you like & trust them, go with it.
- O "Squeeze Pages"
  - ▪ These are what you use to collect people's emails, building the list you can build your strongest relationships with. I have one set up on The Painted Laugh Facebook page, but paid my web designer to do it. I've heard they're easy to set up, but I didn't do mine.
- O Get an Online Shopping Cart, or PayPal Account, or Both
  - ▪ You *personally* need to have good credit to get an Online Shopping Cart that accepts Credit Cards... some companies are www.1shoppingcart.com, www.AuthorizeNet.com (I use this one), and most major banks have them too. They're called "Merchant Accounts" and they usually do have a monthly charge, and take a % of your sales too. (*It's Business! – There's a price to pay when doing any kind of Business!*)
  - ▪ You can *just* accept PayPal, and with PayPal people can use their Credit Cards and send you the money. Plus **you don't need good credit** and they're fees are super minimal.
  - ▪ You can set up a Merchant Account AND accept PayPal. (*That's what I do.*)
  - ▪ Your web designer might know how to do this too, or have certain other companies he suggests... Again, if you like & trust them, give it a shot.
- O Learn some Video Marketing
  - ▪ I gave you some Tips, but really there are some great mentors out there who know a million times more than me. Andy Jenkins is "The Video Boss" and I told you about Mike Koenigs with www.TrafficGeyser.com. Take your time, but make forward progress too. *"Take your time" does not mean in, like, 10 years.*

> ## MISC. STUFF TO KNOW, but not necessary for your immediate success

- You can create a font from your own handwriting for like $10 at www.acrotype.com
- You can shrink your Twitter URLs at www.tinyurl.com so you have a little more space
- You can have an iPhone/iPad/Android app created for you at www.appmakr.com (no "e")... other sites are www.socialjitney.com (*I use this one*) and www.sourcebits.com
- You can look up the Charitable Foundations your fave celebs are hooked into at www.looktothestars.org and see who supports the same causes you're interested in or working with, and see if you can tie your business in with them. (You wouldn't believe how much Painted Laugh Artwork I donate for these Charities to get a tie into my ideal clients with a lot of moola. Win-Win. I get exposure, they get amazing and FREE Art to auction off for a good cause. It's a sincere collaboration and makes the world a better place any way you slice it.
- You can declare new National/International Holidays that support whatever it is you do... this is great to get Media attention for yourself! Declare a Holiday, then alert the Media to it with your pitch about you/your company/your work. Here's how:
  - ✓ Go to http://www.mhprofessional.com/?page=/mhp/categories/chases/content/contact_us.html or email them at chases@mcgraw-hill.com
  - ✓ Note: It takes a long time. Think of one and declare it ASAP, and it'll be in there officially in 18 months or so. *Yep, it really takes that long, but you can still alert the media to it sooner. No harm there.*
  - ✓ Some cool ones include International Minimalist Day, National Lollipop Day, National Lemonade Day, National High-Five Week, National Laughter Week **(that's mine, coming July 2013, thank-you-very-much!)**
- www.pinterest.com is as addicting as Angry Birds, and a ton of fun. You can design your house, wedding, nursery, wardrobe, etc... It's like a vision board online, and I love it. I got most of my images for this book on that site and then contacted the photo owners for permission to use them, and nearly everyone said hells yeah. You can follow me on there: SonjaLandis. (*Original, I know!*)
- Help A Reporter Out (HARO) www.helpareporter.com is a FREE website you can sign-up for, and they alert you when TV & Radio Shows, Magazines, Newspapers, Bloggers, etc... are looking for people for their Media outlets. This equals free publicity, and more expert positioning. Yay! (Note: They email you with requests up to 4 times PER WEEKDAY with the Media opportunities/requests... that's a LOT. Be ready... sometimes it's hella annoying, but completely worth it if you get that ONE big break for *exactly* what you do!
- If you soak beans in water with seaweed in it (you can buy seaweed strips at most supermarkets, except maybe in like, the Bible Belt areas... I mean, *I don't know*...) before you make chili you won't get the farts. (That actually *might* be critical to your success, come to think of it...)

- You can contact www.LivingSocial.com or www.Groupon.com and possibly have your business featured on one of their deals for BIG TIME exposure. If they like you and your business, it's absolutely FREE to work with them, except for the cost of doing business, really. Translation: They take a cut (WIN), you get a ton of exposure, new clients/customers, free advertising and most of the profits (WIN), and whatever company they work with who collects the money takes a little chunk (WIN).
- If you want to write a book and don't have an Agent, Editor, Publisher, Advance $$$, and all that, you can get an ISBN number on Amazon, follow their direction to "format" in for Kindle, Nook, Ipad, etc... and just do it digitally at first... still makes you money AND saves trees! You can also POD (Print-On-Demand) your book, meaning you don't pay to print it until someone places an order for it and pays first. (The quality is getting better – it's still not totally perfect when you go POD -, and the Media doesn't love to latch onto a POD **unless** you're super controversial or get a ton of Buzz going on your own.)
- You should listen to the Beatles' *All You Need is Love* anytime, day or night, loudly. You should sing along. You should dance if there's someone you care about (or at least *know*) nearby. You should hold their hand and look in their eyes when you sing. If that doesn't make you smile and feel like you can do anything in the world, well then you probably don't have a reflection either, you soulless zombie.
- You can self-publish a book with a company called CreateSpace and (AGAIN) make it available for sale on Amazon Kindle for FREE. That's right. So when I say any dipshit can write a book, it's completely accurate these days. The plus: it's easier than ever to tell the world your story, and make a difference. The cons: any dipshit can do it. Proof positive with the book you're holding in your hot little hands right now. Just kidding. I'm no dipshit. WORD!
- Men think it's a woman's dream to find the perfect guy. Shyeah, right. A woman's dream is to eat without getting fat! Duh! And of course, one more piece of Misc. Info you should know is:

RESOURCES AND **RECOMMENDED READING**

5 SMART **WOMEN** YOU SHOULD KNOW ABOUT

- ❖ Lisa Sasevich – Sales
- ❖ Kris Carr – Health and Wellness
- ❖ Danielle LaPorte – Business Development
- ❖ Chalene Johnson – Video Marketing (For Everyone)
- ❖ Katie Freiling – Social Media and Personal Development

5 SMART **MEN** YOU SHOULD KNOW ABOUT

- ❖ Brendon Burchard – Product Development, Growth, Marketing
- ❖ Mark Joyner – Mind Control Marketing, Motivation, and Sales
- ❖ Steve Harrison – Press, PR, Book Publishing, and Media
- ❖ John Assaraf – Mindset, Business Development
- ❖ Andy Jenkins – Video Marketing (Advanced)

Brain Food! Om nom nom...

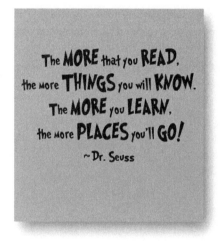

The MORE that you READ,
the more THINGS you will KNOW.
The MORE you LEARN,
the more PLACES you'll GO!
~ Dr. Seuss

www.pinterest.com and again, maybe © Dr. Seuss Enterprises

Books and Writers to Check Out (in alphabetical order):

Bossypants, **Tina Fey**

Chelsea Chelsea Bang Bang, **Chelsea Handler**. You should check out everything by Chelsea Handler if you want to crack up. She. Is. The. Greatest.

Changing the World on a Tuesday Night, **Tammi DeVille**

Crazy Sexy Diet, **Kris Carr**

Driven From Within, **Michael Jordan**

Good to Great, **Jim Collins**

If You Don't Have Big Breasts, Put Ribbons on Your Pigtails, **Barbara Corcoran**

Life Is a Verb: 37 Days to Wake Up, Be Mindful, and Live Intentionally, **Patti Digh**

Life's Golden Ticket, **Brendon Burchard**

Oh The Places You'll Go, **Dr. Seuss**

Outliers: The Story of Success, **Malcolm Gladwell**. *The Tipping Point* is really good too!

Purple Cow, The Dip, Tribes, **Seth Godin**. You should read anything by Seth Godin; he has a great Blog too!

Rich Dad, Poor Dad, **Robert Kiyosaki**

Spilling Open: The Art of Becoming Yourself, **Sabrina Ward Harrison**

The 4-Hour Workweek, **Tim Ferriss**

The 7 Habits of Highly Effective People, **Stephen Covey**

The 12 Secrets of Highly Creative Women, **Gail McMeekin**

The Answer, **John Assaraf** and **Murray Smith**

The Art of Non-Conformity, **Chris Guillebeau**

The Chick Entrepreneur: How to Put Your Business in Higher Heels, **Elizabeth Gordon**

The Last Lecture, **Randy Pausch** (grab a box of Kleenex – this one's a tear jerker but full of Life Lessons!)

The Missing Piece Meets the Big O, **Shel Silverstein**

The Principles of Uncertainty, **Maria Kalman**

Think and Grow Rich, **Napoleon Hill**

Websites and Other (in alphabetical order):

BecomingYou.com – **Sarah Zolecki** (Personal and Business Development)

BianchiRossi.com – **My brother Nick**'s Spring Break Travel Company

ChrisGuillebeau.com – **Chris Guillebeau** (Personal Development)

Colorstrology.com – **Michele Bernhardt** (Astrology, but with Colors)

CrazySexyLife.com – **Kris Carr** (Health & Wellness)

Facebook.com – Like me and my stuff! **What Would Chelsea Do? Book** and **Sonja Landis**

FreePublicity.com – **Steve** and **Bill Harrison** (Press and Media Connections)

Google✚ ("Google Plus") – The new facebook... invite only when I wrote this book. Request your invite now!

KatieFreiling.com – **Katie Freiling** (Personal Development)

LucasRohm.com – **Lucas Rohm**, my web designer, Mission Bay Media (Web Design)

Picnik.com – You can color/contrast/effect your Glamour Shots here for FREE

Pinterest.com – Super creative and fun Social Community, got many of the images for this book on here! Follow me and I'll follow you back! **Sonja Landis**

SethGodin.com – **Seth Godin** (Business Development & Marketing)

ThePaintedLaugh.com – **MY** Art Website!

TrafficGeyser.com – **Mike Koenigs** (Online Presence and Leverage with VIDEOS!)

Twitter.com – Set up your Twitter! Tweet/Follow me and I'll "Follow You" back! **@SonjaSaysLaugh**

WhiteHotTruth.com – **Danielle LaPorte** (Personal and Business Development)

99Designs.com – Bid on Graphic Designers who compete to work for you... Kick-ass!

Photo and Image Credits:

Blahbedy blah blah blah … I put them all in there already with each picture… should I really list them again?? Hmmm, alright. But I'm not doing them in any kind of order. This is straight tomfoolery right here that I'm even listing all this again… Grrrr. Seriously?? I really don't feel like listing all them again. Alright, alright. Alright. I'm just gonna freakin' do it now.

So here's the thing, I had to list www.google.com and www.pinterest.com on a whole bunch of images because that's where I got them, some a long long time ago before this book was even dancing around in my noodle, and others have, like, multiple spots to find them and I'm not sure of the real source or what kind of © is even involved. So to the best of my ability, I have given proper credit and hopefully was able to bring awareness to some cool companies and products for the benefit of my audience, who might want to know about new, cool things, and for the company, whom would probably want to reach new customers they haven't yet. So Like www.bluntcard.com and www.someecards.com and www.taylorsays.com and www.vurtegopogo.com, etc… And I hope the images made you smile. That's what it's all about, lovebug!

In no order whatsoever because I'm tired of this book and my own self: www.google.com, www.pinterest.com, www.emersonwindy.com, www.thepaintedlaugh.com, www.sarahzolecki.com, www.onatuesdaynight.com, www.bluntcard.com, www.someecards.com, www.gracieava.tumblr.com, www.etsy.com, www.fuckyeahdirtyblonde.tumblr.com, www.ColinHarmon.com, www.banksy.com, www.maryelizabethinspire.tumblr.com, maybe my favorite girl ever Chelsea Handler for that tribute to her *Chelsea Chelsea Bang Bang* book (or maybe Borderline Amazing Publishing or Grand Central Publishing… I don't really know), maybe Kris Carr for that *Crazy Sexy Diet* pic I put in there (which you should def read!), Jim Henson for the "Animal" pic probably (and I'm looking forward to the new Muppet Movie coming out! Animal is my son's fave, and was my brother Nick's fave too!!!), NBC Studios for the George Costanza one I think, and maybe Will Farrell for that one, but the source listed www.thebellebeat.com from www.pinterest.com, www.iheartit.com, www.lookonthebrightside.uk.com, www.mollermarketing.com, www.coffee-tea-and-sympathy.tumblr.com, www.beautiful.tumblr.com, www.Louboutin.com, www.bethquinndesigns.com, www.ffffound.com, www.piccsy.com, www.Fitisthenewbeautiful.tumblr.com, www.weblamers.com, www.cafepress.com, www.five-words.tumblr.com, www.dietcokeandasmoke.tumblr.com, www.galadarling.com, Mercedes Benz, www.adsoftheworld.com, www.scissorsandawhisk.blogspot.com, www.cosmopiltan.com, and maybe Dr. Seuss Enterprises.

My brain gets **stronger** everyday because I exercise it.

The **stronger** it gets, **the more money I can make.**

- Robert Kiyosaki Author of *Rich Dad, Poor Dad* and loads of other good stuff too.

AFTERWARD, BUT NOT **THE END**

ALWAYS REMEMBER
YOU ARE **B R A V E R**
THAN YOU BELIEVE
S T R O N G E R
T H A N Y O U S E E M
S M A R T E R
T H A N Y O U T H I N K
& T W I C E A S
BEAUTIFUL
A S Y O U ' D E E V E R
I M A G I N E D

From "SEXYBACK" on www.Pinterest.com

So I guess my Master's wasn't *totally* "useless" when it's all said and done... it just didn't matter AT ALL **like I thought it would.** The best purpose it served was to put me on a path toward everything I didn't want in order to get me (in a long, convoluted way) to what I actually **did**. (I don't recommend the long route!) YOU don't need one to succeed, and it might not be helpful to get you closer to your real dreams in the slightest. And it certainly <u>does not guarantee</u> your dream "job" or lifestyle! If your **true passion** depends on Higher Education, like being a Doctor, Lawyer, or Bridge Engineer... please oh please oh please oh please pursue Higher Education with everything you've got! Just make sure it's your true passion, and make sure you know your motives before you register for Basket Weaving 101. **Take the time to understand where you really want to go, why, and then take the most direct route there.** It may or may not be in College!

YOU

AND YOUR HONESTY (with yourself),

COURAGE (to do something big and unique in the world),

AND ACTION (to move forward)

DETERMINE YOUR SUCCESS!

Someone emailed me this picture, and I had to use it. It brought the biggest smile to my face! I have no idea the source, so whoever owns it, I'm sorry I couldn't give you the proper credit but I would like to high-five you!

You really can do anything you set your mind to

(see picture directly above!)

life is beautiful

Do epic shit

And I'll see you here:

There are **many wonderful things** that will never be done

if **you** do not do them.

- Charles D. Gill

ABOUT THE AUTHOR

:: Sonja Landis ::

Artist, Writer, Mom, Self-Proclaimed Comedian, Entrepreneur, Funny Chick, Drinker of
Cocktails, Teller of Stories, Laugher of Jokes, Lover of Carbs, Loser of Keys

Sonja lives in San Diego, California with her son, 2 idiot dogs (just kidding – she totally loves them
both), and a newly adopted spotted gecko. She runs 2 companies, The Painted Laugh Studio &
Gallery and a Biz Development/Coaching Program for Small Business Owners & Entrepreneurs.
She specializes in Online Marketing, Press & Media Relations, Social Media, Sales Conversion, and
creative Copyrighting. Go to www.SonjaLandis.com and you'll get more Sonja Landis than you ever
could imagine, or probably care for...

Twitter @SonjaSaysLaugh   YouTube: SonjaSaysLaugh

Facebook: www.facebook.com/MyMastersDegreeIsUseless

Facebook: www.facebook.com/SonjaSaysLaugh

Totally Real
(not real at all)
Reviews of this Book

*****

Sonja Landis and I have become really good friends
because of **this book**, and I'm honored to have such a **positive impact** on Women in Business.

- Chelsea Handler *

*Chelsea Handler did not say this

*****

Sonja is amazing, savvy, and smart.
I wish I had her on my show when we were still on the air.

- Oprah Winfrey *

* Oprah Winfrey did not say this

*****

Finally! I am already signed up to the Sonja Landis School of Business.
Her STYLE is Brilliant!

-Warren Buffet *

*You already know that Warren Buffet did not say this. He didn't even imply it a little bit.

*****

Sonja Landis is brilliant, smart, funny, and the most perfect woman I know.
She is my goddess-princess-queen and the love of my life.
I couldn't survive day-to-day without her!

- Sonja's Boyfriend *

*He has said this, maybe not really in so many words, and, like, more with his eyes...

*****

People should buy this book! **You did a really good job, dear.**
And I'm glad you put your brother in it. That was nice.

- Sonja's Mom*

*Sonja's Mom indeed **DID** say this

*****

**What surprises me most about humanity is man. He sacrifices his health in order
to make money. Then he sacrifices money to recuperate his health. And then
he is so anxious about the future that he does not enjoy the present;
the result being that he does not live in the present or the future;
he lives as if he is never going to die, and then dies never having really lived...
But not this woman! Not Sonja Landis!**

-Dalai Lama *

*He said everything but that last part, which he maybe *would* say if he knew me...

*****

I love Sonja Landis! I'm so glad she referred to my fabulous ass in her book.
I'm DEFINITELY inviting her to my wedding, which is, of course, going to be amazing...

- Kim Kardashian*

*Kim Kardashian did not say this.

*Thanks, Kim! So glad that butt x-ray worked out in my favor... otherwise that
joke would've been REALLY embarrassing (for me). P.S. Can I bring a date?? RSVP
for 2, doll, see ya' there!*

*****

**Sonja Landis is beautiful, witty, and intelligent. I'm going to make
her my next girlfriend and whisk her off to Lake Como at once... She might
even be THE ONE, the one to settle me down for good...**

- George Clooney*

*George Clooney did not say this.

***Ohhhh, George, George... had you ACTUALLY said this, I would say I'm flattered
but happily taken. Let's just be friends, and you'll find the right one eventually!***

*****

I don't care if she wrote a book! Is she into older guys and willing to dye
her hair a LOT more blonde???

- Hugh Hefner*

*Hugh Hefner did not say this.

No. And no. But thanks, Hef! XOXO

*****

This book is smart and fun, and addresses so many important issues facing Women and this economy, all the problems arising in the recession... Sonja, she looks so familiar to me?? Was she an Angel for Victoria's Secret with me?? Who else did she model with??

- Heidi Klum, a.k.a "The Body"

*Heidi Klum did not say this, but she really is "The Body"

Heidi! You're so sweet! I get that all the time, actually... but no, I surprisingly was NOT a Supermodel. Please don't be embarrassed – you're not the first to make this same mistake! Kisses!

*****

I didn't read this book! Who the HELL is this chick trying to use MY name to promote HER book?!?!?

- Khloe Kardashian (Odom)*

*Khloe Kardashian did not say this.

Khloe: Obviously! Lighten up, hun. I'm just trying to sell some books here, trying to be funny... don't come after me. I'm devilishly strong and scrappy, but I'm quite sure you could take me. I've seen you rumble on the show, and you look pretty strong... I'm sure we'd actually hit it off and be friends if you got to know me...

P.S. My boyfriend's nephew plays football at the same school where your sisters cheerlead, so you might see me at the games. True story. Don't kick my ass there either, k?!?!

*****

This book is timely intelligent, funny, practical and will inspire people to make a real change in their life, no matter where they're at in this moment. That's such a powerful and universal message!

Plus, didn't I used to party and hook-up with this chick in the late 90s when she used to dance on a beer-tub at a nightclub in Phoenix, paying her way thru college?

- Jamie Foxx*

*Jamie Foxx did not say this.

Jamie- you're too kind and with reference to this book, you're absolutely right: it IS a universal truth we're all in search of. You're an inspiration to so many! Thanks for that. As for the other part, it wasn't me you hooked up with, it was one of my other "beer-tub-girl" friends... this was when you were on In Living Color and I didn't think you were that cute at the time... Boy, if I knew then what I do now!!! Clearly, a big mistake on my part!!!

P.S. I see you at those same football games mentioned above with Khloe Kardashian, Jamie! And you look gOOd. (wink) Holla! Just kidding... I'm totally and happily taken, my jersey is retired.

*****

I'm really happy for you, and Imma let you finish...
I'm sorry, but Beyonce had one of the best videos of all time... ONE OF THE BEST VIDEOS OF ALL TIME!...

- Kanye West*

*Kanye West did not say this.

*Hmmm. Well, Kanye. (long pause...) I agree that Beyonce is truly talented.
Thank you for your kind words and, ummmm, contribution to my book review. I love you, man.*

*****

**This "Sonja"... she needs work done, some Botox or something.
Just a whole make-over would do. Hopefully she sells a lot of books and can take care of this ASAP.**

- Joan Rivers*

*Joan Rivers did not say this.

**Thanks, Joan. Agreed! Getting older is the pits. I'll try and Botox as soon as I can.
Love you!**

*****

I don't care if she wrote a book!!! Did she just "XOXO" at Hef?? Is she flirting with MY Hef?!?!

- Holly Madison*

*Holly Madison did not say this.

*Yes, but no, Holly. Definitely NOT flirting with Hef.
See you in Vegas sometime... Tweet me! (wink!)*

*****

**My books are all better. I did it first. I dance better, sing better, and am in far better shape.
She doesn't even look like she does yoga. Does she study Kaballah?? No, I though not.
Well, I haven't time for this....**

-Madonna*

*Madonna did not say this.

**Whoa, Madge... it's ok. I clearly cannot compete, and certainly don't want a pose off.
Your body is stunning. Big fan. Big. Big. Big fan...**

Take it easy on hydrangeas, will ya?? Geez.

*****

I cannot wait to shred this chick and her book on The Soup. Tune into E!

- Joel McHale*

*Joel McHale did not say this.

Yikes. Be gentle. I think I need some thicker skin for this...

*****

She's just a little bit hot. I'd like to see her take her top off, and I bet she's a real tiger behind closed doors... would she be willing to show her tits and do filthy things on the show while she talks about her really good book??

- Howard Stern*

*Howard Stern did not say this.

Awww Howard, although a few years ago I would've totally jumped on that particular offer, I think that ship has sailed... My boobs are fab, but ya know... I just can't do it anymore... if things don't go well, can I totally change my mind though?!?! I do have bills to pay...
Cool!
Thx bunches!

If you say "gullible" slowly it sounds like "oranges".

Haha... did I getcha?? Did you believe any of those Book Reviews??

What?!?!

Hmmm.. I thought I was so clever & convincing...